Rescued

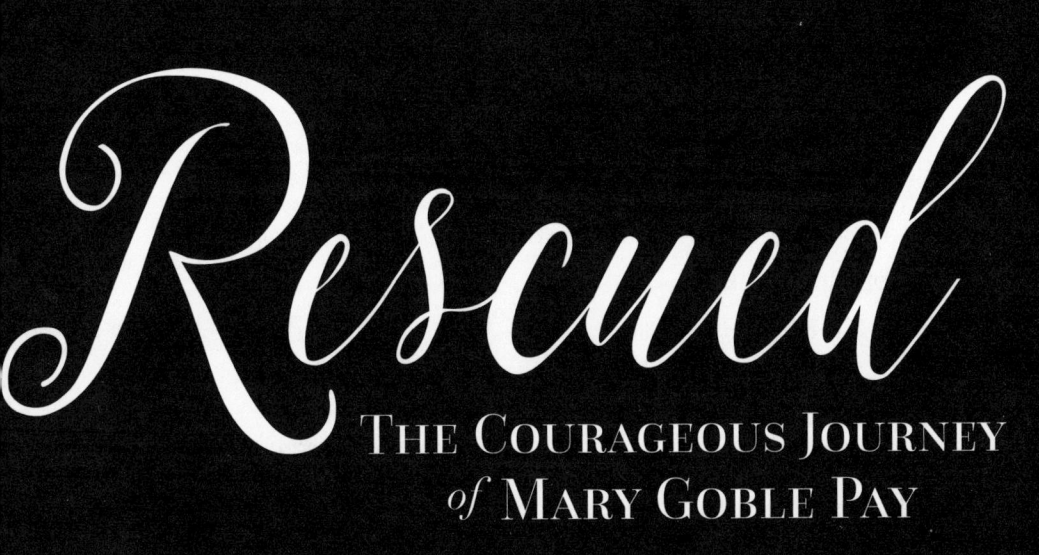

Rescued
The Courageous Journey of Mary Goble Pay

With Introduction and Notes by
Clark B. Hinckley

Published by the Religious Studies Center, Brigham Young University, Provo, Utah, in cooperation with Deseret Book Company, Salt Lake City, Utah.

Visit us at rsc.byu.edu.

© 2021 by Brigham Young University. All rights reserved.

Printed in the United States of America by Sheridan Books, Inc.

DESERET BOOK is a registered trademark of Deseret Book Company.

Visit us at DeseretBook.com.

Any uses of this material beyond those allowed by the exemptions in US copyright law, such as section 107, "Fair Use," and section 108, "Library Copying," require the written permission of the publisher, Religious Studies Center, 185 HGB, Brigham Young University, Provo, UT 84602. The views expressed herein are the responsibility of the authors and do not necessarily represent the position of Brigham Young University or the Religious Studies Center.

Cover and interior design by Carmen Durland Cole

ISBN: 978-1-9503-0405-9

Library of Congress Cataloging-in-Publication Data

Names: Pay, Mary Goble, 1843-1913, author. | Hinckley, Clark B., editor.
Title: Rescued : the courageous journey of Mary Goble Pay / with
  introduction and notes by Clark B. Hinckley.
Description: Provo, Utah : Religious Studies Center, Brigham Young
  University ; Salt Lake City, Utah : Deseret Book Company, [2021] |
  Includes index. | Summary: "Thirteen-year old Mary Goble and her family
  were part of the pioneer overland journey to Utah Territory in the Hunt
  Wagon Company in 1856. They traveled close to the Edward Martin handcart
  company and suffered with them through the cold of Wyoming. The core of
  the book is a transcription of Mary's handwritten memoir with
  annotations that corroborate, correct, and provide context. This
  annotated transcription is bookended by an introduction and epilogue
  that place Mary's story of her journey in the context of her life before
  and after her emigration"—Provided by publisher.
Identifiers: LCCN 2020042369 | ISBN 9781950304059 (hardcover)
Subjects: LCSH: Pay, Mary Goble, 1843-1913. | Hunt Wagon
  Company—Biography. | Mormon pioneers—Biography. | Mormon
  women—Biography. | LCGFT: Autobiographies.
Classification: LCC BX8695.P39 A3 2021 | DDC 289.3092 [B]—dc23
LC record available at https://lccn.loc.gov/2020042369

To my mother,
Marjorie Pay Hinckley,
the granddaughter of Mary Goble Pay,
and my father,
Gordon B. Hinckley,
who instilled within me a love for
my pioneer ancestors and a deep appreciation
for their sacrifices and their faith.

Oh God! Preserve us on the way,
Our lives and health defend;
Let angels guard us night and day,
Until our journey's end.

—From C. W., "Song of the Saint,"
  Millennial Star, 15 December 1855

Contents

ix	Abbreviations and Frequently Cited Sources
xiii	Preface
1	Introduction
17	A Note regarding the Manuscript
23	Selections from the Autobiography of Mary Goble Pay
63	Epilogue
73	Appendix 1: Comparison of Holograph, Larsen Manuscript, Bowers Transcript, and Pay Transcript
97	Appendix 2: Letter from Mary Goble Pay to Samuel S. Jones, 18 October 1908
101	Appendix 3: Comparative Chronology of Willie, Martin, Hunt, and Rescue Company
119	Appendix 4: Hunt Company Camp Journal
145	Appendix 5: Discourse of Brigham Young, 30 November 1856
149	Index
157	About the Editor

Abbreviations and Frequently Cited Sources

Bell	Bell, Stella Jaques. *Life History and Writings of John Jaques: Including a Diary of the Martin Handcart Company*. Rexburg, ID: Ricks College Press, 1978. Excerpts are available on Saints by Sea database and Pioneer Database.
Beecroft	Beecroft, Joseph, Journal, CHL, MS 1915. Excerpts are available on Saints by Sea database and Pioneer Database.
Burton	Burton, Robert T., [Journal] in Journal History of The Church of Jesus Christ of Latter-day Saints, 30 November 1856. This is the camp journal of the Grant rescue party kept by Robert T. Burton.
CHL	Church History Library.
Deseret News	Scanned copies of the *Deseret News* for 1856 are available online at Digital Collections, BYU Library, https://contentdm.lib.byu.edu/digital/collection/desnews1/id/3210.

Hafen and Hafen	Hafen, Leroy R., and Ann W. Hafen. *Handcarts to Zion: The Story of a Unique Western Migration, 1856–1860*. Lincoln: University of Nebraska Press, 1960.
Haven	Haven, Jesse, Journals, 1851–1892, CHL, MS 890. https://catalog.churchofjesuschrist.org/record?id=ad8ab6ae-e172-4510-8f51-7d9643dfdf69&view=browse.
Holograph	Pay, Mary Goble, Autobiography, copy in possession of author. This is Mary's handwritten memoir.
Hunt Journal	Journal History of The Church of Jesus Christ of Latter-day Saints, 15 December 1856, 7–37, CHL, CR 100 37. This entry contains a transcription of the original camp journal of the Jones/Hunt company. https://catalog.churchofjesuschrist.org/assets?id=c875ccf4-42e8-4336-a4a1-608a0e61f880&crate=0&index=322. Another transcription is filed as "Dan Jones Emigrating Company journal," CHL, MS 9395. https://catalog.churchofjesuschrist.org/assets?id=99aa03d3-fd60-461a-a953-841ac9b63291&crate=0&index=1. The original handwritten journal is also in the CHL: "Dan Jones Emigrating Company. Dan Jones Emigration Company journal," MS 1066. https://catalog.churchofjesuschrist.org/assets?id=d81a6c8c-1aad-4231-a121-4242c5cd7df4&crate=0&index=2.
Jones	Jones, Daniel W., *Forty Years Among the Indians*. Salt Lake City: Juvenile Instructor Office, 1890.
Journal History	Journal History of The Church of Jesus Christ of Latter-day Saints, CHL, CR 100 37. The Journal History is essentially a scrapbook containing a variety of documents and entries in chronological order.
Millennial Star	*The Latter-day Saints' Millennial Star* was an official publication of The Church of Jesus Christ of Latter-day Saints in England from 1840 to 1970. From April 1842 to 3 March 1932 it was printed in Liverpool. https://contentdm.lib.byu.edu/digital/search/collection/MStar.
Olsen	Olsen, Andrew D., *The Price We Paid: The Extraordinary Story of the Willie & Martin Handcart Pioneers*. Salt Lake City: Deseret Book, 2006.

Openshaw	Openshaw, Samuel, Diary, CHL, MS1515.
Petrit	Petrit, Sandra Ailey, ed. *Recollections of Past Days: Autobiography of Patience Loader Rozsa Archer*. Logan: Utah State University Press, 2006. https://digitalcommons.usu.edu/cgi/viewcontent.cgi?article=1036&context=usupress_pubs.
Pioneer Database	Previously known as the "Mormon Pioneer Overland Travel Database," this database, maintained by The Church of Jesus Christ of Latter-day Saints, lists all known pioneers who came to Utah before the advent of the transcontinental railroad in 1869. It includes pioneer companies and excerpts from relevant records and documents. https://history.churchofjesuschrist.org/overlandtravel/.
Saints by Sea	Saints by Sea: Latter-day Saint Immigration to America (database maintained by Brigham Young University in collaboration with the Church History and Family History Departments). This database contains names of pioneers whose travel to Utah included travel by ship, together with relevant records and documents. It includes emigrants through 1932. It is available at https://saintsbysea.lib.byu.edu.
Southwell	Southwell, John William, Autobiography. CHL, MS 8243. Excerpts at https://history.churchofjesuschrist.org/overlandtravel/.
Stewart	Stewart, Elizabeth White, [Autobiography], in Workman, Mary Ellen B., comp., *Ancestors of Isaac Mitton Stewart and Elizabeth White* [1978]. CHL, MS M270.1 S8496w, 1978. Excerpts at https://history.churchofjesuschrist.org/overlandtravel/sources/5452/stewart-elizabeth-white-autobiography-in-workman-mary-ellen-b-comp-ancestors-of-isaac-mitton-stewart-and-elizabeth-white-1978.

Preface

I grew up hearing my parents and grandparents tell over and over the story of Mary Goble Pay's journey across the plains. My siblings, my cousins, and I read and reread a typescript of her reminiscences. She was a heroic, almost mythical figure for us, but at the same time she was very real. Our grandfather, Phillip Leroy Pay, was Mary's son, making our connection to our pioneer ancestor seem very close.

As we reached adulthood, we assumed the responsibility of carrying Mary's story to the next generation. In July 1997, the sesquicentennial of the 1847 pioneer company, we chartered a bus, filled it with three generations of Mary's descendants, and traveled the pioneer trail from Casper, Wyoming, to the mouth of Emigration Canyon in Salt Lake City. To prepare for that trip, I made for each of my siblings a copy of the first few pages of Mary Goble Pay's autobiography, to which I added some notes to provide context and clarification to Mary's story. That was the beginning of a project that I returned to at various times over several years and that eventually lead to this book.

Several years later my cousin, Patricia Stoker, obtained a scan of Mary's original handwritten memoir. I was surprised to discover some significant differences between that original document and the typed versions of Mary's autobiography in our possession. In particular, some information in our family copies was not included in Mary's original manuscript.

As with any story told and retold, I realized that certain misconceptions had begun to surround Mary's story. The most common of these was that Mary and her family came by handcart; she has been depicted in both painting and sculpture with "her" handcart and is often portrayed as a member of the Martin handcart company. Yet her family was part of the John A. Hunt wagon company and drove a wagon and ox team; they never pushed or pulled a handcart, though they traveled close to the handcart company and suffered with them through the cold of Wyoming.

My objectives in this book are to document the details of Mary's trek as she described them in her handwritten memoir, place her account in the context of the story of the 1856 emigration, and verify or correct Mary's reminiscence by correlating it with other contemporary records and reminiscences of the events of 1856. This book is not meant to be a definitive account of the 1856 companies that were caught in the winter storms in Wyoming, or even of the Hunt wagon company, of which Mary was a part; although, I have included a significant amount of information on the Hunt company since Mary's story is inextricably intertwined with that of her fellow travelers. It is my hope that this volume will help document and preserve the experience of a thirteen-year-old girl during a few months in 1856, placing her memories of those events in a context that helps the reader better understand what she experienced.

The core of the book is a transcription of Mary's handwritten memoir with annotations that corroborate, correct, and provide context. This annotated transcription is bookended by an introduction and epilogue that place Mary's story of her journey in the context of her life before and after her emigration.

The remainder of the book consists of supplemental materials: a series of sidebars too long to be included as annotations with the text and several appendices with additional information and documents for those who want to go a little deeper. These appendices include a comparison of several versions of Mary's autobiography, a comparative timeline of the principal emigrant companies caught in the storms in October 1856, and a complete transcript of the official camp journal of the Hunt wagon company.

I confess that I have undertaken this work largely for my own benefit, with the thought that it would also be of interest to other descendants of Mary and her family. Perhaps it also may be of some value to others with an interest in the 1856 emigration and particularly to those who may have an interest in the often-neglected Hunt wagon company.

I am indebted to many who have contributed to this work, chief among them my cousin Patricia Henrikson Stoker, who has gathered a wealth of documents and resources on Richard Pay and Mary Goble Pay; my aunts Evelyn Pay Henrikson, Doreen Pay Lloyd, and Joanne Pay Baird, who have for many years kept the story of their grandmother alive; and Christine Bowers and the Bowers family, who have carefully preserved Mary's holograph over the years. This book is much better than it might have been as a result of the excellent suggestions and editing of many individuals at the Religious Studies Center at Brigham Young University, particularly Devan Jensen, Meghan Rollins Wilson, and Cara Nickels. And a special shout-out is due Carmen Cole, who tackled a challenging design problem with talent, skill, and panache. I give them and others their due credit for this book, but claim for myself all its shortcomings and errors.

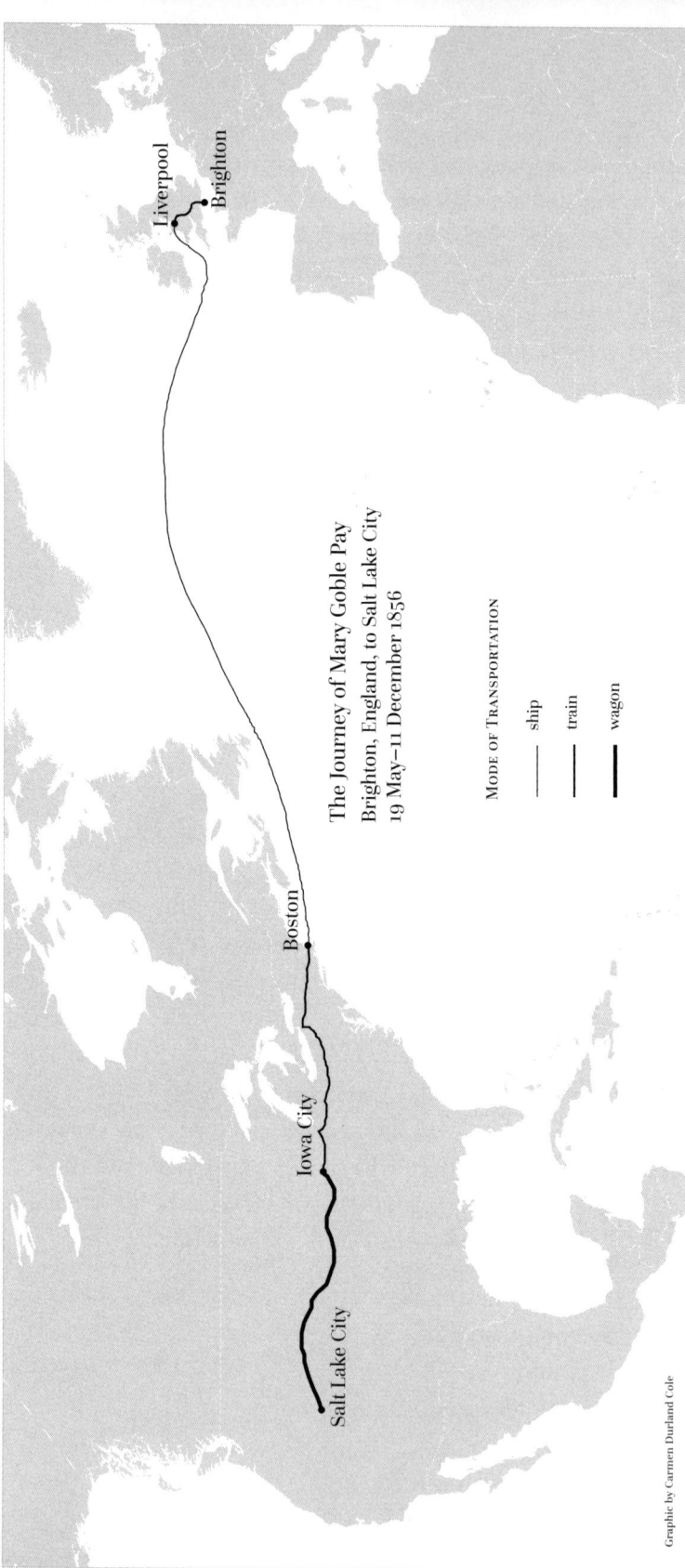

Introduction

Mary Goble had her thirteenth birthday somewhere in the North Atlantic Ocean bound for America. She was the oldest of six children traveling with their parents on the sailing ship *Horizon* from Liverpool to Boston, en route to the Great Salt Lake Valley. Edwin was eleven, Caroline was eight, Harriet was six, James was four, and little Fanny was two. A seventh child—the firstborn—had been born the year before Mary's birth but died at the age of eight months and lay buried back in England. Mary's mother was expecting her eighth child when the family left their home in England and set out for America.

William Goble and Mary Penfold were both born in Sussex, near Brighton, England. They came from farming families but saw better opportunities in the growing seaside resort of Brighton, and it was there that they married in 1841 at St. Nicholas Church, a stately building that was already nearly five hundred years old. Brighton in the 1850s was a prosperous and growing town with a number of trades and a healthy tourist industry. A direct rail

Russell Square in 2020. The Goble family lived at 53 Russell Square before emigrating. Courtesy of Ann H. Rowan.

connection enabled Londoners to make day trips to the Brighton seashore and its famed Royal Pavilion. William Goble was a "greengrocer" (a retailer of fresh fruits and vegetables) and had a home at 53 Russell Square, just about two blocks from the sea. It was a neighborhood filled with merchants and craftsmen. The Gobles' neighbors included a coach maker, two coach painters, a tailor, two butchers, a carpenter, a harness maker, a confectioner, a tinsmith, a saddler, a miller, and a dairyman.[1]

1. See "England and Wales Census, 1851" (database with images), www.familysearch.org, film 101795967, image 390 of 1317; from "1851 England, Scotland

View to the sea from Russell Square. Courtesy of Ann H. Rowan.

Each of William and Mary's seven children was christened at St. Nicholas in a beautiful carved stone font that dates back to AD 1170. Mary, the oldest living child at the time they left Brighton,

and Wales census," database and images, http://www.findmypast.com, citing PRO HO 107, The National Archives of the UK, Kew, Surrey.

St. Nicholas Church, Brighton, Sussex, England, where Mary was christened (and her parents were married). Courtesy of Ann H. Rowan.

was christened on 23 July 1843; Fanny, the youngest, was christened in July 1854.

By the time Fanny was christened at St. Nicholas, however, the Goble family had come in contact with a new religion. William's sister Harriet, who was seven years younger than William, read a copy of the Book of Mormon that had been left with her brother-in-law. She walked five miles the next Sunday to hear an elder of The Church of Jesus Christ of Latter-day Saints preach, reporting, "When the elder stood in the doorway and read the first hymn in the book, the scales of darkness fell from my mind and visions of eternity were opened to my view, and tears of joy fell from my eyes." She was baptized the following Sunday, 3 February 1850, in the River Ouse just outside of Brighton.[2]

---

2. "Harriet Goble" (autobiographical sketch, n.p., n.d.), www.familysearch.org/tree/person/memories/KWJ8-5DZ.

Two more of William's younger sisters, Mary Ann and Matilda, were baptized that same year along with their husbands. William's older sister and her husband, Fanny and John Wood, were baptized in 1852.

Not until March 1855 did William and his wife accept baptism.[3] By then Mary Ann (who was still single) and Matilda (with her husband, Leonard Matless) had already immigrated to America. They had left together in 1853 on the sailing ship *Golconda*, landed in New Orleans, and taken a riverboat up to Keokuk, Iowa. Matilda and Leonard found Keokuk to their liking and remained there, so Mary Ann headed west alone with a company of Saints. On the trek she met a young widower, Thomas Carter, and they were married at Fort Laramie in present-day Wyoming while on their way to the Salt Lake Valley.

Fanny and John Wood sailed from England on the *Samuel Curling* with their six children shortly after the baptism of William and Mary in the spring of 1855. The Woods traveled in a wagon company from Mormon Station, Kansas (near Atchison), to the Salt Lake Valley, arriving in late September of 1855. They settled in Farmington, north of Salt Lake City.

Young Mary and her brother Edwin were baptized as members of the Church in November 1855 in Brighton. Seven months later their father sold the greengrocer business, and the family left Brighton forever.

---

3. FamilySearch shows Mary Penfold's baptismal date as 1 January 1855 and William Goble's as 27 March 1855 (www.familysearch.org).

Mary was only one of an estimated sixty thousand Latter-day Saint emigrants[4] who traveled at least part of the distance from Iowa to Salt Lake City on foot between 1847 and 1869. The first pioneer company, led by Brigham Young, arrived in the Salt Lake Valley in July of 1847. Thirteen more companies of pioneers arrived that same year, the vanguard of one of the greatest mass migrations in modern history.

Emigrants came from five continents and a score of countries. Many of them were poor, and the cost of the journey from Europe, South Africa, India, or Australia stretched their resources. Helping the poor gather to Zion was a constant focus of President Young. It was a daunting challenge; in the early days of the Utah Territory, those who had already immigrated to Utah were struggling to survive and create a viable economy, and there was little surplus to send abroad. In October 1849 the Church created the Perpetual Emigrating Fund (PEF) to assist those desiring to gather to Zion but lacking the financial means to do so. In addition to providing financial assistance, the Church maintained a shipping agency in Liverpool and managing conductors at ports of entry in the United States so emigrants could then be sent on to an outfitting point in the West.

The Perpetual Emigrating Fund was a significant factor in enabling thousands of emigrants to come to Utah, but the need for financial assistance was always greater than the supply. In 1855 the PEF spent $150,000 assisting emigrants from Europe, but drought and grasshoppers in Utah reduced the harvests that fall by more

---

4. Researchers have variously estimated the total from between fifty-one and eighty thousand. See Melvin L. Bashore and H. Dennis Tolley, "Mortality on the Mormon Trail, 1847–1868," *BYU Studies Quarterly* 53, no. 4 (2015): 110n6. The Pioneer Database website, maintained by the Church History Department of The Church of Jesus Christ of Latter-day Saints, includes the most comprehensive list of pioneers who traveled to Utah between 1847 and the coming of the railroad in 1869. Historians estimate that more than sixty thousand individuals emigrated.

than a third, with a related reduction in tithing and donations. Discussions were held regarding curtailing emigration for the following year. On 30 September 1855, President Young wrote to President Franklin D. Richards of the European Mission, "I have been thinking how we should operate another year. We cannot afford to purchase wagons and teams as in times past."⁵ He then proposed an idea that had been considered at least since 1851—the use of hand-drawn carts rather than oxen and wagons. In fall 1851 Brigham and the First Presidency had called for the use of handcarts. "Some of the children of the world have crossed the mountains and plains, from Missouri to California, with a pack on their back to worship their God—Gold. Some have performed the same journey with a wheelbarrow, some have accomplished the same with a pack on a cow," wrote the Presidency. "Families might start from the Missouri River, with cows, handcarts, [and] wheelbarrows," they urged.⁶ But despite such urging, no handcart companies had been organized.

However, with the lack of funds in 1856, the First Presidency determined to organize PEF-funded handcart companies. The plan was laid out in great detail, and the first handcart company, consisting of 274 Saints, set out from Iowa City on 9 June 1856 under the leadership of Edmund L. Ellsworth. A second company of 221 left two days later under the leadership of Daniel D. McArthur. Both companies entered the Salt Lake Valley on 26 September, having traveled thirteen hundred miles in less than seventeen weeks. The

---

5. Brigham Young office files, 1832–1878 (bulk 1844–1877); General Correspondence, Outgoing, 1843–1876; 1855 July–September; CHL, https://catalog.churchofjesuschrist.org/assets?id=821da034-512b-408f-8d52-d723c6c67ffe&crate=0&index=55.
6. "Sixth General Epistle of the Presidency of the Church of Jesus Christ of Latter-day Saints," *Millennial Star* 14, no. 2 (15 January 1852): 23.

third handcart company, sometimes referred to as the Welsh company, consisted of 320 people and 64 handcarts under the direction of Edward Bunker. They left Iowa City on 28 June and arrived in Salt Lake City on 2 October, a journey of ninety-five days.

While these companies reported that provisions were low and strict rationing was required even with significant resupply from the valley, they had, as expected, traveled somewhat faster than most wagon trains, not having the time-consuming burden of caring for a large number of animals. And the mortality rate in the first three handcart companies was similar to that typically experienced by the wagon companies.[7]

The fourth and fifth handcart companies were captained respectively by James G. Willie and Edward Martin. It is their story—the tragedy that befell them as they were caught in early blizzards in Wyoming and the heroism of their rescuers—that is etched into the collective memory of modern Latter-day Saints worldwide. Although the use of handcarts was limited to a total of ten companies between 1856 and 1860,[8] it is the image of handcart pioneers, and particularly of the Willie and Martin companies, that has become the most prominent pioneer image in the minds and hearts of Latter-day Saints. The Willie and Martin companies, together with the William B. Hodgetts and John A. Hunt wagon trains, left late in the season—a full month later than the third handcart company—and about two thousand[9] Saints were caught in the October blizzards. It is their experience

---

7. See Bashore and Tolley. Detailed statistics are in the database referenced in the article.
8. By 1861 the Church and the PEF were able to provide "Church trains"—wagon trains that would go east and pick up emigrants at the staging area and bring them to the valley.
9. The Pioneer Database gives the following numbers for the four companies caught in the early storms: Willie handcart company, 513; Hodgetts wagon company, 173; Martin handcart company, 641; Hunt wagon company, 285—for a total of 1,612 Saints. In addition, the Abraham O. Smoot wagon train, which was carrying freight to Utah, began with about 97 participants, including a number of emigrants, and was caught in the October storms. The site also lists 365 members of the rescue parties, bringing the total to 2,074 Saints.

that has come to symbolize the entire emigration, so much so that the very notion of a modern-day "pioneer trek" is a handcart trek—and for many of the same reasons that handcarts were first used: they are relatively simple and inexpensive.[10]

Mary Goble's short narrative unfolds within the drama of the suffering of these handcart companies. Her family was not a part of the PEF-funded handcart companies: William paid the £35.50 cost of the trans-Atlantic voyage and purchased "two yoke of oxen, one yoke of cows, [and] a wagon and tent" in Iowa, according to Mary, presumably from money he received from the sale of his business in Brighton. But in the weeks following the blizzard of 19 October, the Hunt wagon company, the Hodgetts wagon company, and the Martin handcart company continued to travel close together as they slowly made their way to Salt Lake City with the assistance of rescuers.

Although by late September the hot summer days had faded and the mornings were "cold and frosty,"[11] the weather was still mild when Franklin D. Richards (the thirty-five-year-old member of the Quorum of the Twelve Apostles who, as president of the European Mission, had organized the European immigration in 1855–56) arrived

---

10. Information on the Church website comparing the Philemon C. Merrill wagon company of 1856 and the Daniel McArthur handcart company shows an estimated cost per person of ninety-three dollars for the wagon company and thirteen dollars for the handcart company. "Wagons vs. Handcarts," https://www.churchofjesuschrist.org/media/image/wagons-vs-handcarts-infographic-3defaef.
11. Hunt Journal, 25 September 1856.

in Salt Lake City on 4 October and reported that additional companies of emigrants were still on the plains. Church leaders were already aware that the Smoot wagon company, carrying freight and including several emigrants, was still on the plains, and they had sent resupply wagons to meet that company.[12] The news that four additional emigrant companies were still on the plains came as a surprise to Church leaders in Salt Lake City. "We had no idea there were any more companies upon the Plains," wrote Brigham Young.[13] Consequently, no resupply wagons had been dispatched east to assist them, and by this point they were almost certainly running out of food.

The first members of the rescue party left Salt Lake City in good weather on 7 October. But the mild weather soon yielded to the bitter cold of an early winter. From the first blizzard on 19 October to the arrival of the last stragglers in Salt Lake City on 15 December, snow and freezing temperatures were the constant companions of pioneers and rescuers alike. At least twenty-five members of the Hunt company died on the trail—three of them from the Goble family.[14] More than a hundred members of the Martin company died along the way—exact numbers are difficult to come by because

---

12. The Smoot company encountered relief wagons on 2 October, just beyond the last crossing of the Platte River near where the Hodgetts, Martin, and Hunt companies would be trapped by the snow eighteen days later. Smoot requested additional supplies, and the additional relief wagons reached the company on or about 18 October, just before the blizzard of 19 October; the company was then about three days' travel east of South Pass. They arrived in Salt Lake City on 9 November just ahead of the Willie company. Franklin D. Richards had met resupply teams on 27 and 28 September and counseled them to cache their flour and go on to meet the Willie company, but they apparently turned back before reaching the Willie company. See Richards's report in *Deseret News*, 22 October 1856, and Burton, 30 October 1856).
13. Brigham Young to Orson Pratt, letter dated 30 October 1856, Millennial Star, 19:7, 99.
14. Bashore and Tolley identify twenty-five deaths that occurred after leaving Iowa City, with a possible two others. Deaths which occurred before leaving the staging area are not included in Bashore's and Tolley's analysis. Consequently,

record keeping gave way to survival.[15] The smaller Hodgetts company lost eight to ten members, while the Willie company suffered about seventy deaths. Upon arriving in the valley, Jesse Haven, a returning missionary who served as first counselor to Edward Martin that spring aboard the ship *Horizon*, noted, "When I came out of Emigration Canyon, I shed tears of joy to [be] so near home."[16]

As one pioneer of tens of thousands, Mary Goble did not consider her experience extraordinary. It was not until late in her life that she wrote the simple memoir from which this excerpt is taken.[17] As a reminiscence written nearly fifty years after the events, there are certain details and dates that are at odds with contemporary records and other accounts (many of which are also reminiscences written years after the fact and so not wholly reliable). Yet, on the whole, Mary's recollections were remarkably accurate.

---

their count does not include Mary's little sister who died at the Iowa City campground before the trek began.
15. Bashore and Tolley list the deaths in the Martin company between 76 and 111, a mortality rate of between 12 and 17 percent.
16. Haven, entry dated 15 December 1856.
17. Melvin Bashore notes that the story of the companies caught in the early storms was not generally told until a couple of decades had passed, possibly because the memories were still so painful. See Melvin Bashore, "On the Heels of the Handcart Tragedy: Mormondom's Forgotten 1856 Wagon Companies," *Annals of Wyoming* 68, no. 3 (Summer 1996): 39–40.

Her memoir was written by hand in a ledger dated 1903; it covers fourteen pages, including some entries made at a later date. Her account of traveling from England to Salt Lake City—the focus of this book—covers about four pages.

An edited transcription of her autobiography was included in volume 4 of the six-volume *Treasures of Pioneer History*, published between 1952 and 1957, as well as in volume 13 of the twenty-volume compilation *Our Pioneer Heritage*, published between 1958 and 1977. Typewritten transcripts of her memoir, edited and enlarged, were held by family members, and her story was often told at family gatherings; but it was not until the publication of her memoir in the 1974 collection *A Believing People*[18] that her story became widely available. Portions of her autobiography have since been printed in a variety of publications, and President Gordon B. Hinckley—her

---

18. Richard H. Cracroft and Neal A. Lambert, eds., *A Believing People: Literature of the Latter-day Saints* (Provo, UT: Brigham Young University Press, 1974). The compilation was reviewed by Eugene England in *BYU Studies* in 1975. In his review, England opined that most of the literature of the Latter-day Saints was not "great" in the sense that the writing of Milton or Shakespeare is great: "I don't believe [God] held his highest spirits in reserve that they might come forth in the latter days as our great writers, certainly not as Ernest Hemingways or Norman Mailers, but not even as Miltons or Shakespeares, who, whatever they may have contributed to the aesthetic pleasure and sensitivity or even moral and philosophical insight of us all, most likely have brought few, if any, souls to Christ. That after all, is God's first concern and would seem to be his primary mission for his 'highest spirits.' Yes, I believe God held in reserve the sensitive and articulate Apostle Parley P. Pratt—and also the plain-spoken and stubbornly courageous handcart pioneer, Mary Goble Pay—both of whom produced good (not 'great') literature that is included in this anthology; but the reason they were sent to us in in these latter days and the reason I most value them is not for the greatness of their writing, but for the greatness of their lives." Eugene England, "A Believing People: Literature of the Latter-day Saints, ed. Richard H. Cracroft and Neal E. Lambert," *BYU Studies* 15, no. 3 (1975): 367.

grandson-in-law—mentioned her story in general conference. A search of the *Ensign* magazine shows at least a dozen references to Mary Goble, including four in general conference addresses.[19] Her story has been recounted or mentioned in manuals for Primary, Young Women, and Aaronic Priesthood. Just as the Martin and Willie handcart pioneers have become the icons of the entire pioneer migration, this simple narrative of Mary Goble Pay stands out as an iconic account from the ill-fated companies of 1856.

This volume endeavors to provide background on the events mentioned by Mary, together with dates and names that help flesh out the story, and to put it all in context with the scene that unfolded across the plains of Wyoming, particularly in October and November of 1856, when there were over fifteen hundred pioneers (in four companies) strung out across two hundred miles of high prairie—the Willie company farthest west and the Hodgetts, Martin, and Hunt companies to the east. At the same time, rescue teams were traveling east with assistance, and express riders were moving back and forth as fast as the weather and their horses would allow, trying to make sense of what was happening and get information and help to where they were needed most. The rescuers, caught in the same storms as the emigrants, found their own lives in jeopardy, and the

---

19. Gordon B. Hinckley, "Our Mission of Saving," general conference, October 1991; Gordon B. Hinckley, "The Faith to Move Mountains," general conference, October 2006; "Experiences Worth Remembering" (Brigham Young University devotional address), 31 October 2006; Virginia H. Pearce, "Faith Is

movement of so many groups in various directions makes for a complex story.[20]

But much of the power of Mary's narrative lies in its simplicity and brevity: a father and mother with six young children and a seventh on the way, converts of just a few months, leave their comfortable home in England in May. In December, the father and four badly frozen but surviving children arrive in the Salt Lake Valley with the mother's frozen body in the wagon; three children lie buried on the trail. Mary's narrative endures as a moving story of a young girl and her family who were willing to sacrifice everything for the gospel.

Mary's father, William Goble. Courtesy of FamilySearch.

---

the Answer," general conference, October 1994; and Elaine S. Dalton, "It Shows in Your Face," general conference, April 2006.
20. There were many other travelers on the road in September and into October of 1856. See Sidebar 4: Life on the Trail.

A Note regarding the Manuscript

Several different, though very similar, typewritten transcriptions of Mary Goble's autobiography have been in private hands as well as in the Church History Library for many decades. It was not until 2011, when Patricia Henriksen Stoker (a great-granddaughter of Mary Goble) was researching the life of Mary Goble Pay for a chapter in *Women of Faith in the Latter Days*, volume 2,[1] that Mary's original handwritten manuscript became available to a broader group. This manuscript is referenced herein as the holograph, and it has some significant variations from the typewritten manuscripts. The holograph is written in a ledger book and begins with the title "Nephi, City Feb. 1903."

---

1. Christine B. Bowers, Virginia H. Pearce, and Patricia H. Stoker, "Angels Shall Minister unto You," in *Women of Faith in the Latter Days, Volume 2: 1821–1845*, ed. Richard E. Turley Jr. and Brittany A. Chapman (Salt Lake City: Deseret Book, 2011).

The pages of Mary's history match the handwriting found on a letter written by Mary Goble Pay in the Church History Library (included herein as appendix 2). The ledger book was in the possession of Dora Bowers (a granddaughter of Mary Goble Pay) and her husband, Jacob Bowers, who graciously allowed Patricia Stoker to scan the pages. A careful transcription was done by Ashley and Christine Bowers and, independently, by Patricia Stoker.

Another handwritten manuscript of Mary's autobiography is contained in a small notebook with a printed cover: "Collegiate No. 1110 Composition Book." The notebook measures 6½ by 8¼ inches and contains fifty sheets. On the cover is the name Vera Pay Larsen. Inside the front cover is a handwritten note: "Vera Pay Larsen was Mary Goble Pay's granddaughter who prevailed upon Mary Goble to write her story." The handwriting is not that of Mary Goble Pay but presumably is that of Vera Pay Larsen. This manuscript is in the possession of the author and is referenced herein as the Larsen manuscript.

There are at least two versions of early typewritten transcripts of Mary's autobiography. One consists of ten pages, single-spaced. It carries the title "LIFE OF MARY GOBLE PAY." Copies of this document were produced on a mimeograph machine and circulated among the descendants of Phillip LeRoy Pay, Mary's youngest son. Some extant copies have handwritten notes that appear to be in the handwriting of Phillip LeRoy Pay's wife, Georgetta Paxman Pay. This document is referenced herein as the Pay transcript and is virtually identical to the Larsen manuscript, suggesting that the Larsen manuscript may have been the basis for the Pay transcript (and for other copies of Mary's autobiography including those mentioned below).

A second typescript version consists of nineteen typewritten pages on lined paper, each with the word "FAMILY" printed in the right-hand top corner of odd-numbered pages, and "HISTORY" printed in the left-hand top corner of even-numbered pages. The document is titled "Mary Goble Pay." It is in the possession of the Jacob Bowers family. This transcript is referenced herein as the Bowers transcript. It has only minor variations from the Larsen manuscript and the Pay transcript.

At least three additional transcripts, essentially identical to the Pay transcript, are housed in the Church History Library.[2]

The Larsen manuscript and the various transcripts are nearly identical in content and structure and include information not contained in the holograph. Three types of differences are noted:

- The Larsen manuscript and the various transcripts reflect punctuation, spelling, and sentence structure changes designed to make the document more readable and to flow somewhat better than the holograph.
- The Larsen manuscript and the various transcripts alter the order of certain portions of the holograph. This was probably done to try and place some events in their proper sequence.
- The Larsen manuscript and the various transcripts add some important information not contained in the holograph. This additional information may be based on oral information that was known to family members.

A side-by-side comparison of the excerpts of the holograph relating to Mary's emigration experience and corresponding excerpts of the Larsen manuscript, the Pay transcript, and the Bowers transcript is included as appendix 1. Published versions of Mary's autobiography appear to be derived from the Larsen manuscript or one of the mentioned typescripts.[3]

---

2. The three are catalogued as MS 11650, MS 13811, and MS270.07 P343 199.
3. Cracroft and Lambert give their sources as Leon Pay, "members of the Pay family," and "Arthur Coleman's compilation, *Pay-Goble Pioneers of Juab County, Utah*, copyright 1968 by Arthur Coleman."

The text of this book follows the holograph, edited for punctuation, spelling, and sentence structure (including the insertion of words to clarify meaning). Additional information found in the Larsen manuscript and the Bowers and Pay transcripts is included in the annotations and for convenience is referred to as being from the Larsen manuscript, although these additions are also in the Pay transcript and, with one exception, the Bowers typescript.

Many of the details of Mary's narrative can be corroborated using other primary contemporary documents and reminiscences, though occasionally there is some variance in the details in the accounts of participants. Some of the information included in the annotations and notes is based on what may be considered primary documents but not firsthand accounts—essentially recollections of children and grandchildren based on family stories. And some details are educated guesswork. For example, there is no primary contemporary source that identifies Willow Springs as the place where Mary was lost in the snow, but a review of the position of the company each day makes this the likely spot because it fits the description of events.

Chronology of Mary Goble's Journey

1843	2 June	Born in Brighton, Sussex, England.
1855	5 Nov	Baptized a member of The Church of Jesus Christ of Latter-day Saints.
1856	19 May	Leaves Brighton and travels to London.
	20 May	Travels from London to Liverpool.
	25 May	Sails from Liverpool on board the *Horizon*.
	2 June	Turns thirteen years old while at sea.
	30 June	Disembarks in Boston.
	4 July	Passes through Buffalo, New York, via train.
	8 July	Arrives at Iowa City, Iowa.
	13 July	Joins fifth wagon company organized at Iowa City under Captain Dan Jones.
	19 July	Sister Fanny (age twenty-three months) dies of measles at Iowa City.
	1 Aug	After twenty-five days in Iowa City, leaves with the Hunt wagon company at 4:00 p.m. and travels two miles.
	28 Aug	Hunt company arrives at Florence.
	31 Aug	Hunt company leaves Florence.
	24 Sept	Baby sister Edith born.
	7 Oct	Goble's wagon damaged in cattle stampede.
	19 Oct	Arrives at the last crossing of the Platte; blizzard during the night.
	2 Nov	Around this date, Mary is lost in snow, and her toes freeze.
	3 Nov	Edith dies at Greasewood Creek.
	5 Nov	Arrives at Devil's Gate. Brother James dies while at Devil's Gate.
	11 Dec	Mother dies between Big and Little Mountains at about 4:00 in the afternoon; arrives in Salt Lake about 9:00 p.m. at night.
	12 Dec	Toes amputated by Dr. Williams.

Selections from the Autobiography of Mary Goble Pay

I, Mary Goble, was born in Brighton, Sussex, England, June 2, 1843. My father was William Goble, son of William and Harriet Johnson Goble. My mother was the daughter of John and Sarah Penfold. My childhood days were spent the same as most children['s]. When I was in my twelfth year, my parents joined the Latter-Day Saints. On November the 5th I was baptized. The following May we started for Utah. We left our home[1] May 19, 1856.

---

1. William Goble is listed in the 1851 Brighton post office directory as a "Fruiterer & Greengrocer" living at 53 Russell Square in Brighton, Sussex.

We came to London the first day,[2] the next day came to Liverpool,[3] and [then we] went on board the ship *Horizon* that evening.[4] It was a sailing vessel.[5] There were nearly nine hundred souls on board.[6]

We sailed on the 25th. The pilot ship came and tugged us out into the open sea. I well remember how we watched old England

2. The Brighton station of the London, Brighton and South Coast Railway was located less than a mile from the Gobles' home. The fifty-five-mile trip to London ended at London Bridge station. The next day the Gobles left London from Euston Station, about three miles from London Bridge, on the West Coast Main Line for Lime Street Station in Liverpool.
3. Liverpool was a principal Atlantic seaport of England. The *Liverpool Mercury* for 21 May 1856 includes notices of commercial ships sailing to Port Natal (South Africa), Australia, Trieste, Genoa, Naples, Le Havre, and Constantinople. The paper also notes preparations for a great public holiday on 29 May 1856 to celebrate the end of the Crimean War. The celebrations were to include "a public demonstration of the children educated in the town" and a regatta on the River Mersey. In the mid-nineteenth century, Liverpool rivaled London in wealth. Nathaniel Hawthorne, already a successful and well-known author, was the US consul in Liverpool in 1856.
4. By Mary's accounting, the family arrived in Liverpool on Tuesday, 20 May 1856, and boarded the *Horizon* that evening. The ship left the dock on Friday, 23 May, and anchored in the river. It was brought into open sea and officially began the voyage on Sunday, 25 May.
5. By 1856 steamships were crossing the Atlantic regularly. The passage by steamship took about ten days, compared to thirty-seven days for the *Horizon*, but the price of passage on a steamship was far too expensive for most immigrants. It was not until 1863 that a majority of immigrants traveled to America by steam. See Edwin C. Guillet, *The Great Migration: The Atlantic Crossing by Sailing-ship Since 1770*, 2nd ed. (Toronto: University of Toronto Press, 1963); and *The Geography of Transport Systems*, https://transportgeography.org/?page_id=2135.
6. The *Horizon* was a US registered ship of 1,775 tons under the command of Captain W. Reed. It sailed from Liverpool on 25 May 1856 with 856 Saints and arrived in Boston on 30 June 1856 after thirty-seven days at sea. While nearly 75 percent of the passengers received financial assistance from the PEF, the Gobles paid their own way, sending nine pounds in advance to reserve their passage and paying the remaining 26.50 pounds upon boarding. They held

fade from sight. We sang, "Farewell, Our Native Land, Farewell."[7] While we were in the river, the crew mutinied and they were put ashore, and another crew came on board.[8] They were a good set of men.[9] When we were a few days out, a large shark followed the vessel. There was one of the saints who died; he was buried in the sea.[10] We never saw the shark any more.

---

ticket 144. The ship register lists William Goble as a "Greengrocer" and Mary Goble, age twelve, as "Spinster." For rosters and information on each ship see Saints by Sea database at https://saintsbysea.lib.byu.edu. Original source information in British Mission Emigration Register (BMR), CHL.

7. See Sidebar 1: "Farewell, My Native Land, Farewell."
8. The mutiny took place while the *Horizon* was still in the River Mersey and before the captain had boarded. Heber Robert McBride remembered, "When we got out on the river and cast anchor . . . the sailors and the ship officers got into a quarrel and began to fight. This almost frightened some of the emigrants to death, but the first mate ran into the cabin and came out facing the men that was after him with a pistol in each hand caused them to stop very quick. He told them the first man that moved he would shoot him down. He stood there and kept them back till a signal of distress was sent up and it was hardly any time before boats came alongside with policem[e]n and all the crew was put in irons and taken to shore." Heber Robert McBride, Autobiography, 5–9, 15–16, CHL. John Jaques also recorded the incident. See *Millennial Star* 18, no. 26 (28 June 1856): 411–12.
9. John Jaques was particularly complimentary of Captain Reed: "As regarding our Captain, I can speak nothing but good. . . . He acted like a man and a gentleman." John Jaques to Orson Pratt, 22 July 1856, in *Millennial Star* 18, no. 35 (30 August 1856): 556.
10. The death mentioned by Mary was probably that of George Baker, age twenty-seven, from Brighton, who died on Sunday, 1 June 1856. See Sidebar 2: Life aboard the *Horizon*.

"Farewell, My Native Land, Farewell"

In his autobiography written in 1912, John Southwell, a passenger on the *Horizon*, recalled:

> The 22nd [of May 1856], the last morning we were to see our native shores, dawned upon us in all its grandeur. It was fair and fine, not a breeze to interrupt our successful boarding [of] the grand old ship as she lay all ready underway out in the open waters, ready to receive her precious cargo. I will give you an idea by the few lines that Elder Silas [Cyrus] H. Wheelock had hastily composed for the departing Saints to sing [up]on leaving our land. It is but a few lines and ran as follows:
>
> Our gallant ship is underway to bear me out to sea.
> And yonder floats the steamer gay that says she waits for me.
> The seamen dip their ready oars as ebbing waves oft tell,
> To bear me swiftly from the shore, my native land, farewell.
>
> As the gay decorated steamer towed us to the *Horizon*, sound was heard above all other noise and din, "My Native Land, Farewell."[1]

The hymn quoted by Southwell was actually written by W. W. Phelps and is titled "The Gallant Ship." It was included in the 1835 hymnal published in Kirtland and appeared in subsequent hymnals through 1940. The hymn was also included in the 1851 edition of the Manchester Hymnal. It was written as a hymn for missionaries departing for their fields of labor. The third verse reads as follows:

> I go to break the fowler's snare,
> To gather Israel home:
> I go the name of Christ to bear
> In lands and isles unknown.
> And when my pilgrim feet shall tread
> On land where darkness dwells,
> Where light and truth have long since fled
> My native land farewell.[2]

Saints gathered on the dock sang the hymn for Brigham Young and his companions as they set sail for their first mission to England in 1840. A revised version of the hymn was included in the script of the British Pageant, *Truth Will Prevail*, in which the lyrics were adapted to reflect the departure of emigrants rather than missionaries.

Mary recalled the hymn sung on the day of the *Horizon*'s departure as "Farewell, Our Native Land, Farewell." There does not appear to be any hymn or poem with that exact title or refrain, but the December 1855 issue of the *Millennial Star*, printed and distributed just after Mary's baptism, includes a poem entitled "Song of the Saint" by "C. W." Its theme is the departure of emigrants headed

---

1. Southwell, 11.
2. "Collection of Sacred Hymns, 1835, 64, The Joseph Smith Papers, https://www.josephsmithpapers.org/paper-summary/collection-of-sacred-hymns-1835/66.

to Zion and it begins with the phrase, "Farewell, my native land, farewell":

> Farewell, my native land, farewell,
> Thou has no charms for me—
> I go with Zion's sons to dwell—
> 'Mongst noble men and free.
>
> Chorus:
> Across the mighty deep we roll,
> With spirits bold and free:
> Blow gently gale, fill every sail,
> And speed us o'er the sea.
>
> Adieu to priestcraft, pomp, and pride,
> Oppression and distress;
> I go the laws of God t'abide,
> With those the Lord will bless.
>
> No earthly tie or sympathy
> Shall cause my heart to grieve;
> I leave them all most joyfully,
> With Saints of God to live.
>
> What is the joy the world affords,
> What are its happiest hours,
> Compared with those consoling words,
> "Eternal lives are yours?"
>
> I'll go to Zion's peaceful vale,
> And learn celestial love,
> And there prepare with gods to dwell
> In realms of bliss above.
>
> Oh God! preserve us on the way,
> Our lives and health defend;
> Let angels guard us night and day,
> Unto our journey's end.[3]

Such poetry was popular with the early Saints. On 2 May 1856, two days before the *Thornton* sailed from Liverpool with members of the Willie company on board, a twenty-year-old girl in the company composed a poem entitled, "Farewell to Thee, England." It was published in the *Millennial Star* on 25 June 1856 and includes this final stanza:

> Yet why should the thought of this last adieu grieve me,
> Oh cannot I part from my own native shore,
> Yes, the voice of the Spirit is bidding me leave thee,
> Farewell then forever, I'll view thee no more.[4]

The author, Emily Hill, traveled with her sister and survived the ordeals of the Willie company, arriving in Salt Lake on 9 November 1856. Years later Emily penned the hymn "As Sisters in Zion."[5]

Before the pilot tug left the *Horizon* on 25 May, Franklin D. Richards and others held a last meeting on deck, addressing the Saints and leaving a blessing. Years later, Josiah Rogerson wrote, "The clarion tenor of W. C. Dunbar and the sweet baritone of John Kay in the 'O ye mountains high, Where the clear blue sky, Arches over the vales of the free' is still ringing in the ears of every passenger [there] that day on the *Horizon*."[6]

---

3. C. W. "Song of the Saint," *Millennial Star* 17, no. 50 (15 December 1855): 800.
4. Emily Hill, "Farewell to Thee, England," *Millennial Star* 18, no. 25 (21 June 1856): 400.
5. Emily Hill Woodmansee, "As Sisters in Zion," in *Hymns* (Salt Lake City: The Church of Jesus Christ of Latter-day Saints, 1985), no. 309.
6. Josiah Rogerson, "Martin's Handcart Company, 1856," *Salt Lake Herald-Republican*, 13 October 1907.

After we got over our seasickness, we had a nice time. We would play games and sing songs of Zion. We held meetings, and the time passed happily.[11] When we were sailing through the banks of Newfoundland, we were in a dense fog for several days. The sailors were kept night and day ringing bells and blowing foghorns. One day I was on deck with my father, when I saw a mountain of ice in the sea close to the ship. I said, "Look, father, look." He went as white as a ghost and said, "Oh, my girl." At that moment the fog parted. The sun shone bright till the ship was out of danger, [t]hen the fog closed on us again.

We were on the sea six weeks when we landed at Boston.[12] We took the train[13] for Iowa City, where we had to get our outfit for the plains. It was the end of July.[14]

---

11. See Sidebar 2: Life aboard the *Horizon*.
12. On Monday, 30 June 1856, the steam tug *Huron* towed the ship to Boston's Constitution Wharf and the passengers disembarked, ward by ward. They had been at sea thirty-seven days. John Jaques recorded on Sunday, 29 June 1856, "While the doctor was passing the passengers, the captain and his family came on board. Meeting on the main deck at 3 p.m. Three cheers for the captain and three for the officers and crew. The captain responded and said that this company of emigrants was the best he had brought across the sea. He complimented them on their good behavior and said that we sang, 'We'll Marry None But Mormons,' and he said he would say that he should 'Carry None But Mormons.'" He added, "Seventeen years later [1873] Captain Reed crossed the continent, not by handcart, but by rail, and called on a few of the emigrants residing in Salt Lake, whom he carried across the Atlantic. Very much pleased was the old gentleman to see them." Bell, 100, 106.
13. Like ship travel, train travel was uncomfortable, with the emigrants traveling in boxcars while sitting on their luggage.
14. Jesse Haven reported a temperature of 108 degrees in Iowa City on 22 July 1856. Haven, 22 July 1856. Traveling in such hot weather, it is not too surprising that the emigrants could not appreciate the risk of leaving so late in the season.

2

Life aboard the *Horizon*

Mary and her family spent over five weeks aboard the *Horizon*. Elder Edward Martin, returning from a mission in England, was the leader of the company of Saints. Jesse Haven, returning from a mission in South Africa, was first counselor, and George P. Waugh, a British convert, was second counselor; John Jaques was historian.[1] Both the *Thornton*, which sailed from Liverpool on 4 May 1856 and arrived in New York on 14 June 1856, and the *Horizon* were hired by Franklin D. Richards to carry Latter-day Saint emigrants. Most of the passengers on these two ships were organized into one of the four companies that were caught in the early storms in Wyoming, with the majority of the *Thornton* passengers becoming part of the Willie company, and those of the *Horizon* joining the Hodgetts, Martin, or Hunt companies.

With 856 passengers plus the crew aboard the *Horizon*, space was tight: "The berths for two passengers are about six feet long by four feet four inches wide, lined up like horses' mangers, two in height."[2]

The Saints were organized into nine wards, each with presiding officers. Wards combined for Sunday services, but each ward held prayer meetings each morning and evening as well as fellowshipping meetings. Edward Martin wrote to Franklin D. Richards, saying, "I make it my business to visit every part of the ship six or seven times a day."[3]

A bugle was sounded each morning at 5:00 a.m. (later changed to 6:00 a.m.) and each evening at 10:00 p.m. The passengers prepared their meals in the galley. John Jaques wrote, "Cooking for 800 hungry people at one galley is not a trifling affair, especially when each family or person has a private pot or dish."[4]

Four couples were married during the voyage. Four children were born, including Nancy Horizon Wilson and William Horizon Paxman. John Jaques notes six deaths, including little Nancy Wilson and two other children who died in Boston Harbor before disembarking.[5]

After a few days at sea, Jaques reported that "the children make themselves happy, both above and below deck. Marbles, skipping ropes, and all the available paraphernalia of childhood's games are called into request. The older boys amuse themselves by tugging at the ropes with the sailors. So merrily we live together."[6]

The first day at sea was smooth and quiet. "But what a change the next day," wrote Jaques. "Seasickness changed our countenances to a pitiful, pallid hue. . . . Such a

---

1. See Olsen, 219; *Millennial Star* 18, no. 34 (23 August 1856): 542.
2. Bell, 79.
3. Edward Martin to Franklin D. Richards, 29 May 1856, in *Millennial Star* 18, no. 26 (28 June 1856): 411.
4. John Jaques to Franklin D. Richards, 29 May 1856, in *Millennial Star* 18, no. 26 (28 June 1856): 412.
5. See Bell, 102.
6. *Millennial Star* 18, no. 26: 413.

worshipping of buckets and tins, and unmentionable pans, I shall not attempt to describe."⁷

A few weeks after arriving again on terra firma, Jaques reported, "I think, altogether, that we, on the *Horizon* had as agreeable a voyage as most emigrants are favored with. We had an occasional rough breeze . . . and split a sail or two, but not a single storm did we experience." Still, he concluded, "I like the beginning and end of a sea voyage better than another part of it."⁸

---

7. *Millennial Star* 18, no. 26: 413.
8. John Jaques to Orson Pratt, 22 July 1856, in *Millennial Star* 18, no. 35 (30 August 1856): 555.

3

Train Travel

Ships, train passage, and outfitting were all handled by Church officials and the Perpetual Emigrating Fund Company. Josiah Rogerson, later a member of the Martin company, recorded these details of the journey from Boston to Iowa City:

> July 2, we took the cars from Boston to Albany, passing through Buffalo on the glorious Fourth of July.
>
> We reached Cleveland, Ohio, on the 5th, passing Kirtland with its temple in the night.
>
> Sunday evening, July 6, we arrived at Chicago, Ill., where we stayed all night.
>
> Monday, July 7, we left Chicago early in the morning and arrived at Rock Island in the evening.
>
> Tuesday, July 8, we crossed the Mississippi by a ferryboat and then took the cars from Davenport for Iowa City, reaching there the same evening.
>
> Wednesday, July 9, we were employed in unloading and hauling our luggage to the camping ground on "Iowa hill," three and one-half miles northwest of Iowa City, Ia., the outfitting point for that year's Mormon emigration.¹

Joseph Beecroft noted that the Saints "rode in luggage vans and our seats were our luggage which was in our way. We were uncomfortable in some things, but comfortable in mind. We were cramped with being confined, some slept in the carriages and some laid down on the ground."² The emigrants sometimes slept in warehouses arranged by the Church. The night of 6 July they stayed in a warehouse in Chicago. Beecroft describes the scene: "The floor of the extensive warehouse was [so] covered with human beings that there was scarcely room to put your foot down without treading on someone."³

---

1. Rogerson, *Salt Lake Tribune*, 30 November 1913, 11.
2. Beecroft, entry for 2 July 1856.
3. Beecroft, entry for 7 July 1856.

On the first of August[15] we started to travel with our ox teams unbroke[n], and we did not know a thing about driving oxen.[16] My father had bought two yoke of oxen, one yoke of cows, a wagon, and [a] tent. He had a wife and six children. Their names were Mary, Edwin, Caroline, Harriet, James and Fanny.[17]

My sister Fanny broke out with the measles on the ship,[18] and when we were in Iowa Campground,[19] there came up a thunder

15. The Hunt Journal records that the fifth wagon company left on 1 August 1856 with about three hundred emigrants and fifty-six wagons.
16. Many of the Saints had little or no experience working with oxen, and the learning curve was necessarily steep. Ruth May Fox recalled, "Imagine if you can these would-be drivers, who had, perhaps, never seen a Texas steer before, go though the procedure for the first time of yoking their cattle. Truly no rodeo could match the scene. The men had to be instructed in this art and some did not learn very quickly." Ruth May Fox, "From England to Salt Lake Valley in 1867," *Improvement Era*, July 1935, 408–9, 450. Managing unruly oxen was both challenging and dangerous. The Hunt Journal notes that on 7 October some of the oxen began stampeding. "Sister Esther Walters . . . was knocked down and so badly injured that she expired in a few minutes . . . leaving a babe four weeks old." The Gobles' wagon was broken in the stampede and had to be repaired before they could continue.
17. The Goble children (and their ages on the trek) were Mary, born 2 June 1843 (age thirteen), died 25 September 1913; Edwin, born 29 September 1845 (age eleven), died 27 October 1913; Caroline, born 21 January 1848 (age eight), died 14 February 1922; Harriet, born 31 May 1850 (age six), died 20 June 1890; James, born 23 May 1852 (age four), died 6 November 1856 (at Devils Gate, Wyoming); Fanny, born 23 July 1854 (age two), died 19 July 1856 (at Iowa City, Iowa). Edith was born 23 September 1856, died 3 November 1856 (near Greasewood Creek, present-day Horse Creek in Wyoming).
18. In a letter addressed to Franklin D. Richards, written and mailed from Boston on 30 June, John Jaques reported, "The measles appeared on board on May 29 and many of the children and some adults have had the disease, but we have to record no deaths from it." However, the next day, while still in Boston, Jaques recorded, "Bro. Palmer's child died this evening of the measles." Bell, 106.
19. The campground was about three and a half miles northwest of Iowa City in an area now preserved as Mormon Handcart Park located in present-day Coralville, Iowa (just off Mormon Trek Boulevard). Several interpretive signs have been placed in the park. Saints from the *Horizon* arrived on 8 and 9 July; Saints from the *Thornton*, most of whom were organized into the Willie

storm. It blew down our shelter made with hand carts and some quilts. The storm came and we were there in the rain, thunder and lightning.[20] Fanny got wet and died the 19th of July 1856. She would have been two years old on the 23rd of July. The day before we started on our journey, we visited her grave.[21] We felt awful to leave our little sister there.

---

company, had arrived at the campground on 26 June and did not leave until 15 July, so for six or seven days, there were over sixteen hundred emigrants living in the campground.

20. The storm occurred the day the emigrants from the *Horizon* arrived at Iowa City, and the Gobles apparently had not yet purchased a wagon, and so found shelter where they could.

    Elizabeth White Stewart, a member of the Hunt company, recorded, "When we completed our journey to Iowa City we were informed that we would have to walk four miles to our camping ground. All felt delighted to have the privilege of a pleasant walk. We all started, about 500 of us, with our bedding. We had not gone far before it began to thunder and lightning and the rain poured. The roads became very muddy and slippery. The day was far advanced and it was late in the evening before we arrived at the camp. We all got very wet. The boys soon got our tent up so we were fixed for the night, although very wet." Elizabeth White Stewart, "Autobiography," in *Ancestors of Isaac Mitton Stewart and Elizabeth White*, comp. Mary Ellen B. Workman (n.p., 1978), excerpt at https://history.churchofjesuschrist.org/overlandtravel/. Peter Howard McBride remembered, "The night we arrived in Iowa, there was the worst storm I ever have experienced, thunder, lightning, rain coming down in torrents. There were wagons to take our bedding and luggage to camp three miles away, but we had to walk. Parents lost their children and children their parents, but we finally got settled in tents for the night." "Journal of Peter Howard McBride," in *Our Pioneer Heritage*, comp. Kate Carter (Salt Lake City: Daughters of Utah Pioneers, 1970), 13:360–63, excerpts available at https://saintsbysea.lib.byu.edu/mii/account/553.

21. A plaque in the Mormon Handcart Park identifies a pioneer burial ground where some of those who died at the campground were buried.

Life on the Trail

The initial phase of the trail covered 270 miles from Iowa City to Florence, Nebraska, which the company covered in twenty-eight days, an average of 9.6 miles per day.

Traveling across Iowa in August, the emigrants' biggest challenge was the heat, with temperatures exceeding 100°F. Cooler temperatures in September were broken by a heat wave in early October: Jesse Haven recorded a thermometer reading of 112½°F on 3 October, well past the peak of summer heat. The effect of the heat was often compounded by deep sand, requiring additional exertion for both those in handcarts and those in wagons. "It pulled the very pluck out of one," remembered John Jaques.[1] The heat was interrupted by fierce thunderstorms unlike anything these European Saints had ever seen. John Southwell of the Martin company remembered this experience: "[There was] one of the most horrible electric storms I ever saw, . . . accompanied by hail and rain. It proved a perfect deluge. . . . In the space of ten minutes the roads became almost impassable, and oh, what a scene to behold. . . . Our tents were rolled up in the wagons. After everyone was drenched and many were unable to move out of their tracks, the captain gave orders to pitch camp and set up the tents the best [we] could in the mud."[2]

The company spent two days in Florence before setting out for Fort Laramie (not to be confused with present-day Laramie, which is 82 miles southwest of Fort Laramie), a distance of 522 miles. The company arrived after forty-one days of travel, an average of 12.7 miles per day. Nine days after arriving at Fort Laramie, the blizzard of 19 October struck, stopping the company for several days near the last crossing of the Platte.

The pioneer trail, particularly across Nebraska from Florence to the last crossing of the Platte, was heavily traveled, even well into October, and the company often met other travelers along the road. The Hunt Journal notes that on a single day, 2 October, "A company of mule teams, carrying soldiers, etc., bound for Fort Laramie, passed the brethren at 10 o'clock a.m. An hour later, they met a company of people with ox-teams, who were on their way back to the States from Utah and who gave an account of the poverty of the people there. At noon, the brethren met a company of soldiers and mule teams from Fort Laramie." Franklin D. Richards and his companions, traveling by horse carriage from Florence to Salt Lake City, report passing not just the four principal emigrant companies, but the Smoot train, Porter Rockwell with several freight wagons,

---

1. Jaques, *Salt Lake Daily Herald*, 19 January 1879; see also Olsen, 278.
2. Southwell, 11; see also Olsen, 278.

a freight wagon train delivering merchandise to Gilbert and Gerrish, and the Jacob Croft company with Saints "principally from Texas and the Cherokee lands."[3] Parley P. Pratt and a group of missionaries were among those traveling east during those same months. Captain William F. Raynolds of the US Army Corps of Topographical Engineers, traveling with Jim Bridger, arrived at the North Platte near the last crossing of the Platte on 11 October 1856, eight days before the Hunt company arrived there. He compared the emigrant trail to "any turnpike in the east." He reported that "we were seldom out of sight of some vehicle upon this great highway.... The Platt road is truly a national thoroughfare."[4]

The members of the company were frequently concerned about Indians. On 5 September the company met "some Californians who reported that Almon W. Babbitt's company had been attacked by Indians and that two men and a child had been killed; one woman (a Mrs. Wilson) was missing."[5] Babbitt, former president of the Kirtland Stake and then secretary of the Territory of Utah, was in charge of four wagons carrying government property to Utah. The wagons were attacked by Cheyenne Indians while encamped at Buffalo Creek (20 miles west of Wood River) in Nebraska. Babbitt was not with the wagons during the attack, but later he and two others were attacked and killed by Indians east of Fort Laramie. Thomas Margetts and James Cowdy, along with their wives and a child, were killed by Indians on 6 September.[6]

Samuel Openshaw wrote, "The Indians are very hostile about here. They have attacked some of the immigrants who have passed through this season, and rumor says that some have been murdered."[7] The killings were done by a small band of Cheyenne Indians in retaliation for the killing of some Cheyennes by US Army troops.

The daily schedule was marked by the sound of a bugle: 5:00 a.m., call to arise and have breakfast; 6:00 a.m., public prayers; 7:00 a.m., break camp. The bugle was sounded for lunch, again to signal the end of lunch, then later to signal a halt for the evening. At 8:00 p.m. the bugle sounded for public prayers, and at 10:00 p.m. it called to put out fires and retire. Years later John Southwell recalled, "Oh, that bugle, that awful

---

3. Franklin D. Richards and Daniel Spencer, "Journey from Florence to G. S. L. City," *Deseret News*, 22 October 1856.
4. Captain William F. Raynolds, *Report on the Exploration of the Yellowstone River* (Washington, DC: United States Army Corps of Engineers, 1868), 70–72.
5. Hunt Journal, 5 September 1856.
6. See Richards and Spencer, "Journey from Florence to G. S. L. City," *Deseret News*, 22 October 1856.
7. Samuel Openshaw diary, CHL, MS 1515, 7, entry for 13 September 1856; see also Olsen, 296.

bugle. How disgusting it was to the poor, weary souls who needed rest."[8]

There was the occasional birth along the way. In the Hunt company, Jane Walters was born 6 September, little Edith Goble was born on 24 September, and Ruth Jones was born on 6 October. But the travail of giving birth under such circumstances robbed the events of much of their natural joy: Jane's mother was trampled in a cattle stampede on 7 October; little Jane died on 5 November; Edith Goble lived less than seven weeks and died on 3 November; Edith's mother died on 11 December. Of the three babies born on the trek, two died on the trail, along with their mothers.

Death was a part of trail life, even before the storms of late October. On 4 October, sixty-four-year-old Susannah Bruner (or Bryner) died about 1:30 in the morning. She was buried at 8:00 a.m., and the company was underway by 8:30. Then just before midnight of the 4th, ten-week-old Marinda Nancy Pay, daughter of Richard and Sarah Pay, died. On 6 October, John Turner, age forty-two, died. The next day Esther Walters died. On 9 October, John Joseph Wiseman, age five, died "from bodily weakness."[9]

Despite many difficulties and challenges, there were some pleasant occasions along the Iowa and Nebraska trail. Often, encounters with local settlers were contentious, but John Southwell recalled that on one occasion, "the singing of the young ladies at [the] evening service drew the attention of the kinder disposed people, and in the morning they brought butter and milk into camp and expressed themselves as being pleased with the way we conducted ourselves traveling through the country. At their request, on breaking up camp we sang the handcart song, which pleased them. They bid us success on our journey."[10]

For these British Saints, many from the crowded and dirty cities of industrial England, the wide-open prairies and fresh air of Iowa and Nebraska were a marvel: "We . . . traveled through a beautiful country where we could stand and gaze upon the prairies as far as the eye could carry, even without being able to see a house. [I] thought [about] how many thousands of people [there are] in England who have scarce room to breathe and not enough to eat. Yet all this good land [is] lying dormant, except for the prairie grass, to grow and decay, which if men would spread themselves and obey the commandment of God to replenish the earth, instead of thronging together in cities and towns and causing the air to be tainted with stinks and giving rise to disease, what a blessing it would be."[11]

---

8. Southwell, 23.
9. Hunt Journal, 9 October 1956.
10. Southwell, 21.
11. Openshaw, 9.

We traveled through the States until we got to Council Bluffs.[22] I think that was the name. It is in Wyoming.[23] Then we started on our journey of one thousand miles over the plains. It was about the first of September.[24] We traveled from 15 to 25 miles a day. We used to stop one day in the week to wash, and [we] rested on Sunday to hold our meetings. Every morning and night we were called to prayers by the bugle.[25]

The Indians were very hostile as they were on the warpath, so our Captain J[ohn] Hunt[26] had us make a dark camp. That was to stop and get our supper, then travel a few miles and not light any fires but camp and go to bed. The men had to travel all day and guard every other night.[27]

22. The company passed through Council Bluffs, Iowa, and ferried across the Missouri River on 27 August 1856, to Florence, Nebraska (now part of Omaha, Nebraska). It covered a distance of 277 miles in twenty-two days, an average daily distance (including rest days) of 12.6 miles.
23. Council Bluffs, Iowa, is located on the east bank of the Missouri River, just across from present-day Omaha, Nebraska. Known as Kanesville from 1848 to 1852, Council Bluffs was considered the beginning of the pioneer trail for both Mormons and other immigrants heading west.
24. The company "commenced to move out of Florence at 8 o'clock a.m." on 31 August. Hunt Journal, 23.
25. See Sidebar 4: Life on the Trail.
26. The company was originally led by Dan Jones (returning from a mission to Wales and distinct from the Daniel W. Jones of the rescue party), but he was asked to travel west with Franklin D. Richards. On 10 August, John Alexander Hunt was appointed captain and on 14 August, Dan Jones left the company. Hunt was born 16 May 1830 in Gibson County, Tennessee. He was baptized in March 1843, and in 1850 he made the journey to Utah. In 1852 he was called on a mission to England and returned in 1856 with many of his converts. He was twenty-six years old, single, and a returning missionary when he was captain of the wagon train. He died in St. Charles, Idaho, in 1913, the same year that Mary Goble Pay died.
27. There was good reason to be concerned about American Indians, because a band of Cheyennes had killed several travelers in retaliation for the killing of some Indians by US troops. The Hunt company first learned of the killings on 5 September when the company met "some Californians who reported that

One night the cattle were in the corral made with the wagons, when one of the guards saw something crawling along the ground. All in a moment the cattle started. It was a noise like thunder. [The guard] shot off his gun when the animal jumped up and ran. It was an Indian with a buffalo robe; he dropped it. Mother and us children were sitting in the tent. Father was on guard. I tell you, we thought our time had come. But Father came running to tell us not to be scared for everything was all right.

We traveled on till we got to the last crossing of the Platte River.[28] That was the last walk I ever walked with my mother. We caught up with the handcart companies that day. We watched them cross the river.[29] There were great lumps of ice floating down the river. It

---

Almon W. Babbitt's company had been attacked by Indians and that two men and a child had been killed." Hunt Journal, 5 September 1856. See Sidebar 4: Life on the Trail.

28. Though generally referred to as the last crossing of the Platte, this is actually a crossing of the North Platte River near present-day Casper, Wyoming, about 625 miles west of Florence, Nebraska. The company covered this distance in 48 days, averaging 13 miles per day. See Sidebar 6: Last Crossing of the Platte.

29. The Hunt company reached the ford about two p.m. on 19 October. The Hodgetts wagon company "had just forded when we arrived and the handcart company crossed directly afterwards." Hunt Journal, 19 October 1856. Years later, Elizabeth White Stewart of the Hunt company remembered: "We finally reached the last crossing of the Platte River. We were then about 500 miles from Salt Lake. Our company camped on the east side and the handcart company passed over that night. All our able-bodied men turned out to help them carry women and children over the river. . . .The snow fell six inches during that night; there were thirteen deaths during the night. . . . The snow continued falling for three days." Stewart, excerpt at https://history.churchof jesuschrist.org/overlandtravel/sources/12707365103905597270-eng/stewart -elizabeth-white-autobiography-in-workman-mary-ellen-b-comp-ancestors -of-isaac-mitton-stewart-and-elizabeth-white-1978?firstName=Elizabeth &surname=White.

was bitter cold. The next morning there were fourteen dead in camp through the cold.[30] We went back to camp and went to prayers. They sang, "Come, Come, Ye Saints, No Toil Nor Labor Fear." I wondered what made my mother cry. That night my mother took sick. The next morning my little sister was born. It was the 23rd of September. We named her Edith. She lived six weeks and died for want of nourishment and was buried at the last crossing of the Sweetwater.[31]

My mother never got well. She lingered till the 11th of December, the day we arrived in Salt Lake City, 1856. She died between the Little and Big Mountains. She was buried in Salt Lake City Cemetery. Her age was 43 years. She and her babe lost their [lives] gathering to Zion in such a late season of the year.[32]

30. Accounts regarding the number of deaths vary, but Elizabeth Horrocks Jackson of the Martin company recalled, as Mary did, that fourteen died during the night of 19–20 October. *Leaves from the Life of Elizabeth Horrocks Jackson Kingsford* (Ogden, UT, n.p. 1908).

31. Mary combines some events in this paragraph that were actually several weeks apart. Edith was born 24 September in Nebraska; the Hunt company reached the last crossing of the Platte twenty-five days later, on 19 October, having traveled approximately 350 miles since Edith's birth. On that day they helped the Martin company cross the Platte among lumps of floating ice and slush. A storm began just as the Martin company completed the crossing, with a fierce wind, snow, sleet and hail. On 20 October the Hunt Journal records, "This morning the ground covered with snow which prevented the company from moving." The Hunt company stayed at the crossing for three days, trapped by the storm. They began fording the Platte about 1:00 p.m. on 22 October and camped about a mile beyond the crossing. Edith died at Greasewood Creek on 3 November. See Sidebar 5: Edith Goble.

32. The Larsen manuscript includes an additional paragraph at this point in the narrative: "We had been without water for several days, just drinking snow water. The captain said there was a spring of fresh water just a few miles away. It was snowing hard, but my mother begged me to go and get her a drink. Another lady went with me. We were about half way to the spring when we found an old man who had fallen in the snow. He was frozen so stiff, we could not lift him, so the lady told me where to go and she would go back to camp for help for we knew he would soon be frozen if we left him. When she had gone I began to think of the Indians and looking and looking in all directions.

We traveled in the snow from the last crossing of the Platte River. We had orders to not pass the handcart companies. We had to keep close to them so as to help them if we could. We began to get short of food. Our cattle gave out. We could only travel a few miles a day. When we started out of camp in the morning, the brethren would shovel the snow to make a track for our cattle. They were weak for the want of food as the buffaloes were in large herds by the road and ate all the grass.[33]

I became confused and forgot the way I should go. I waded around in the snow up to my knees and I became lost. Later when I did not return to camp the men started out after me. It was 11:00 p.m. o'clock before they found me. My feet and legs were frozen. They carried me to camp and rubbed me with snow. They put my feet in a bucket of water. The pain was terrible. The frost came out of my legs and feet but did not come out of my toes." See Sidebar 6: Lost in Snow.

33. The express riders from the rescue company made contact with the Hunt company on the night of 28 October just about a mile from the last crossing of the Platte, where they had been trapped by snow after crossing the river. Traveling with the assistance of a few members of the rescue party, it took the company eight days to reach Devil's Gate. The Martin company traveled a few miles ahead of the Hunt company. The Hodgetts company was between the Martin company and the Hunt company (see Hunt Journal, 5 November 1856), although their location is sometimes difficult to ascertain since there is no separate camp journal for the Hodgetts company. In a report to Brigham Young dated 2 November 1869, George Grant states, "Met br. [Edward] Martin's company at Greasewood creek, on the last day of October; br. [William B.] Hodgett's company was a few miles behind." George D. Grant, "The Companies Yet on the Plains," *Deseret News* [Weekly], 19 November 1856, 293. Appendix 4 gives a comparative chronology of the Willie, Martin, and Hunt companies, as well as this initial rescue party. See also Sidebar 8: The Rescue.

During this difficult stretch of road, the Hunt company draft animals became so weak that it was difficult for the company to make much progress through the snow and cold. The Hunt Journal reports that on 3 November "fourteen or fifteen oxen were left on the road."

Edith Goble

Mary Penfold Goble was approximately four months pregnant when she and her family boarded the *Horizon* in May 1856; by the time the Hunt company left Iowa City, she was six months pregnant. She gave birth to little Edith on 24 September in Nebraska. Edith died forty-one days later on 3 November at 9:00 p.m. while the company was camped on Greasewood Creek.

Edith was twenty-five days old when the blizzard hit the company on 19 October. From that day until Edith's death, the weather was unrelenting: "October 20: This morning the ground was covered with snow. . . . It commenced snowing again at 3 p.m. October 21: The snow was about 8 inches deep. October 23: The weather was very cold and frosty. . . . The camp was still detained because of snow. By this time several of the cattle had died. October 24: A very cold northwest wind was blowing, and the snow was quite deep. October 25: The snow drifted by the effect of a cold and strong wind. October 28: The weather continued cold."[1]

The company resumed travel on 29 October; fresh snow fell on 1 November, and on 2 November the snow was "6 or 7 inches deep, and the weather was very cold."[2] The next evening little Edith died. Presumably she was buried either that night or the next morning; the company did not leave camp until 3:00 p.m. the next day.

Regarding Edith's death, Mary (Goble Pay) later wrote, "When my little sister died at Sweet Water [Greasewood Creek], Bro. [Richard] Pay helped my father when she was buried by the roadside. I felt like I couldn't leave her, for I had seen so many graves opened by the wolves. The rest of the company had got quite away when my father came back for me. I told him I could not leave her to be eaten by the wolves, it seem[ed] too terrible. But he talked to me and we hurried on."[3] Mary may have called the camp where Edith died "Sweet Water" because Greasewood Creek was the only source of good water along a twenty-five-mile stretch of road between the North Platte River and the Sweetwater River.

Three of Mary's granddaughters—Evelyn Henrikson, Dorene Lloyd, and Joanne Baird—related the following regarding the death of Mary's sister, Edith:

> Our dad [Mary's youngest child, Phillip LeRoy Pay] told us that when the company moved on, William noticed that Grandma wasn't with them. He found her sitting on Edith's grave crying. She told her father that she couldn't leave her baby sister there to be dug up and eaten by

---

1. Hunt Journal, 28 October 1856.
2. Hunt Journal, 2 November 1856.
3. Holograph, 7.

Opposite page: *My Father Came Back for Me*, by Julie Rogers.

wolves like she had seen before. Her father told her that Edith was now in Heaven and she was ok. Grandma knew all that but still could not leave the grave. So he helped Grandma gather rocks and sagebrush to cover the grave. Then they built a fire on top of the rocks so that wolves couldn't smell the body and the baby would be safe. Only then could she force herself to travel on.[4]

The concern about wolves was genuine. Elizabeth White Stewart recorded, "Another sad event, one night a father and little son went out for wood to make a fire. They never returned. One leg was found in the father's boot. Wolves had eaten them."[5] Jonathan Stone of the Martin company was also apparently attacked and killed by wolves near the last crossing of the Platte.

---

4. Evelyn Henrikson, Dorene Lloyd, and Joanne Baird, "Richard Pay and Mary Goble," 11 November 2018, unpublished document in possession of the author.
5. Stewart, https://history.churchofjesuschrist.org/overlandtravel/sources/5452/stewart-elizabeth-white-autobiography-in-workman-mary-ellen-b-comp-ancestors-of-isaac-mitton-stewart-and-elizabeth-white-1978.

6

Lost in Snow

The Larsen manuscript and the Pay and Bowers transcripts include information, not included in the holograph, that describes the incident when Mary was lost in the snow and her feet became frozen.

This incident probably took place on 2 November. On 1 November it began to snow again and "the road led through poisonous creeks of water."[1] The company camped that night at a location with no water. The next day, Sunday, 2 November, the company traveled just four miles and camped near Willow Springs, "where the snow was 6 or 7 inches deep, and the weather was very cold."[2] Mary may have walked toward Willow Springs in search of fresh water on the evening of 2 November.

Patience Loader of the Martin company explains the desire for fresh water in her account describing her arrival at Willow Springs: "We traveled on and got into camp. There were five or six brethren [from the rescue company] with their wagons camped there. They had been and got quantities of wood and they had already made a dozen big fires for us and there was plenty of lovely water. That was a great treat to us for we had had nothing but snow water and that did not taste good as we had to melt it over the campfire. It tasted of sagebrush, and sometimes of cedar wood smoke."[3] If this incident took place on 2 November, as supposed, little Edith died the following day.

---

1. Hunt Journal, 1 November 1856.
2. Hunt Journal, 2 November 1856.
3. Petrit, 79.

Last Crossing of the Platte

Travelers bound for Oregon, California, or Utah all traveled essentially the same route from Nebraska to central Wyoming. The route followed the Platte River to the confluence with the North Platte, then followed the south bank of the North Platte to present-day Casper, Wyoming. At Casper, the trail crossed the North Platte and continued through Wyoming to South Pass.

The river crossing near Casper is often referred to as the last crossing of the Platte. The water could be "swift, deep and shockingly cold,"[1] making the crossing treacherous. When the vanguard pioneer company arrived at the crossing in 1847, Brigham Young had a ferry constructed, and the Church continued to operate the ferry each season until John Baptiste Richards succeeded in building a bridge in late 1852.

Richards's toll bridge was downriver (north) about a mile from the ferry crossing. It was generally known as Reshaw's Bridge, derived from Richards's French pronunciation of his name. Near the bridge was a cluster of buildings that included a trading post, several small houses, and a military post referred to in the Hunt Journal as "Ft. Bridge." The military post was officially Camp Davis, named after secretary of war Jefferson Davis.

Passing by here in the summer of 1856, J. Robert Brown, traveling with a trading company, described the scene: "There are several very good log buildings here; these are used as a store, dwelling houses for the traders, blacksmith shop, etc. There are about thirty lodges belonging to the Crows and Sioux, the soldiers live in lodges also; there are only fifty-eight of them here now."[2]

During the summer the bridge toll was six dollars per wagon. Although the toll may have been less late in season, it was apparently beyond the reach of the participants in the Hunt company, let alone the Perpetual Emigrating Fund Company's handcart companies. However, one fifty-six-year old man from the Martin company, after seeing the crossing, determined to take the bridge: "Bro [Jonathan] Stone an aged gentleman who crossed the River on the Bridge to avoid wading was benighted and supposed[ly] lost his way [since] he never came into camp again but this morning an English boot with a [human] foot in it was brought to Camp by Bro Jos[eph] Mc Murran [McMurrin] which were identified as all that was left of Bro Stone. It is supposed that being very fatigued [he] had lain himself down to rest and was attacked and eaten by wolves."[3]

Mary recounts the plight of Stone in her 1908 letter to Samuel Stephen Jones (see appendix 2), where she recalls that her future husband, Richard Pay, was the one who discovered the body.

---

1. "Crossing the North Platte River," https://wyohistory.org/encyclopedia/crossing-north-platte-river.
2. J. Robert Brown, Journal, Western Americana Collection, Beinecke Rare Book and Manuscript Library, Yale University Library, New Haven, CT, quoted in "Reshaw's Bridge" at https://wyohistory.org/encyclopedia/reshaws-bridge.
3. William Lawrence Spicer, Reminiscences, undated, CHL, MS 14688, entry for 20 October 1856.

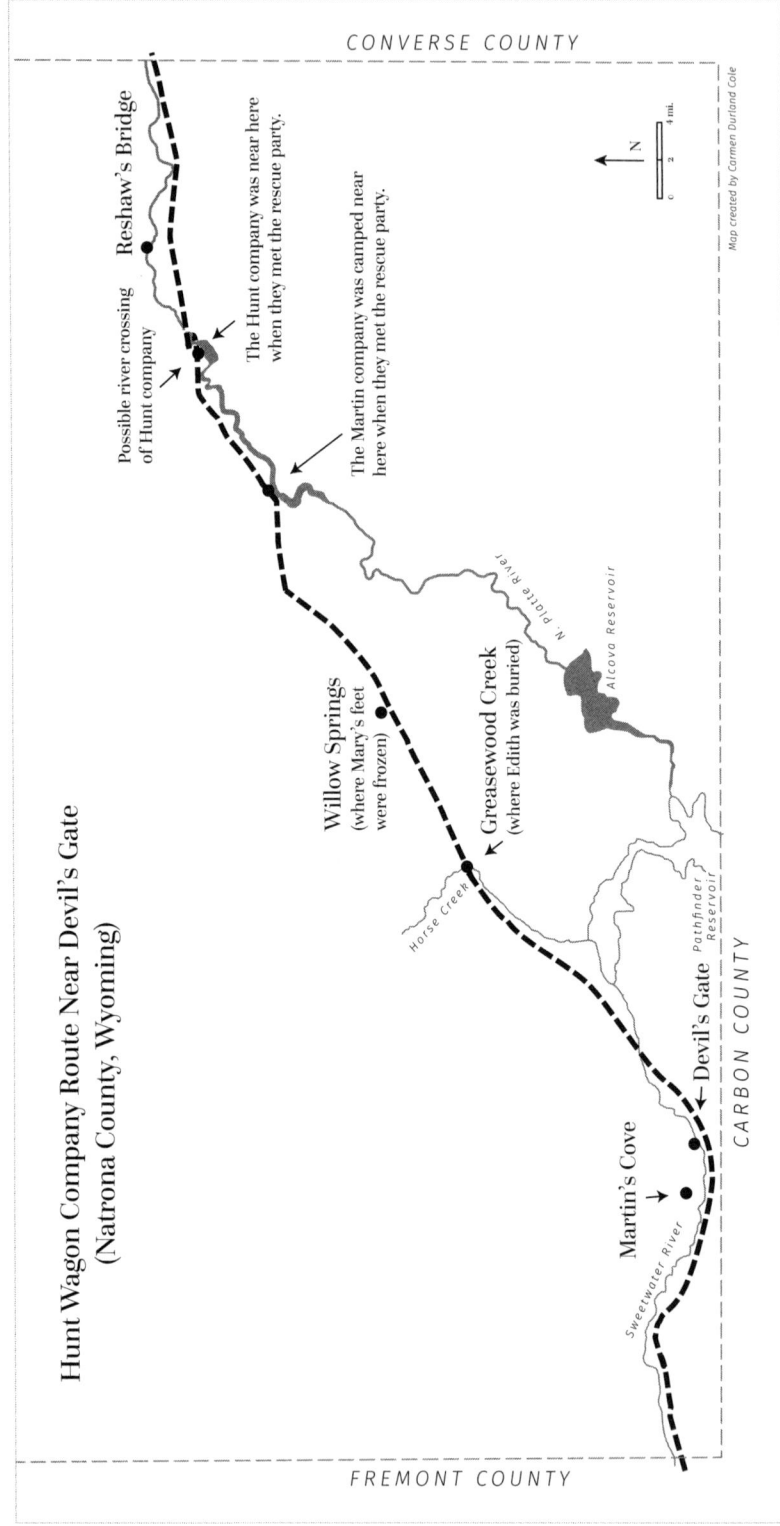

The Rescue

The first three handcart companies left Iowa City on 9 June, 11 June, and 28 June, respectively, with a total of 820 Saints. At about the same time that these companies left Florence, Nebraska, resupply wagons left Salt Lake City headed east. The first resupply wagons met the first handcart company at Deer Creek, about thirty miles east of present-day Casper, Wyoming, on 31 August, forty-two days after the handcart emigrants had left Florence. Additional resupply wagons met the companies at Pacific Springs, just west of the Continental Divide near South Pass. While there were some logistical issues with these first companies—they were larger than anticipated, handcarts were not ready for them when they arrived in Iowa City, and the resupply provisions "were rather short"[1]—the coordination with the resupply trains was remarkably smooth.

When the third handcart company arrived in Salt Lake on 2 October, there was a festive mood in the city—it was thought that the emigration season had ended successfully and that the handcart experiment had proved workable. Until Franklin D. Richards arrived two days later, no one in Salt Lake apparently knew that there were still about sixteen hundred emigrants on the trail for whom no resupply trains had been sent. His report ignited urgent action—the Willie company was already forty-eight days out from Florence and probably already near the end of its food supply.

The initial rescue party left Salt Lake City on 7 October, the same day that a cattle stampede damaged William Goble's wagon and killed Esther Walters while the Hunt company was near the Platte River just west of Scott's Bluff in present-day Nebraska—more than five hundred miles separated the rescuers from the Hunt company. This initial rescue party was under the direction of George D. Grant. The forty-four-year-old Grant had arrived in Salt Lake on 4 October with Franklin D. Richards after completing his service as a missionary in England. The party consisted of about fifty men, six of whom had returned from England with Grant just three days earlier and consequently knew some of the emigrants still on the plains. The men had between sixteen and twenty-two wagonloads of food and supplies, each drawn by four mules. Numbers vary in different accounts, perhaps because the composition of the party was not entirely static.

On 14 October, when this first rescue company was just east of Fort Bridger, Grant sent four express riders (Joseph A. Young, Cyrus H. Wheelock, Steven Taylor, and Abel Garr) east on horseback to locate the companies. When the storm came on the evening of 19 October, the rescue party was just east of South Pass and the Hunt company was trapped in the snow on the east side of Platte, about 170 miles away.

The express riders met the Willie company on the 19th, and the main rescue company reached them two days later. Grant left six teams with the Willie company and set out with eight wagons

---

1. "Official Journal of the First Handcart Company," reprinted in Hafen and Hafen, 213.

in search of the Martin, Hodgetts, and Hunt companies. Meanwhile, the express team was still heading east to locate the companies, with instructions to go to Devil's Gate, where it was expected the companies would be found. Grant met up with the express team at Devil's Gate on 27 October, with no sign of the missing companies. Grant then sent Joseph A. Young, Dan Jones and Abel Garr further east in search of the emigrants.

Young, Jones, and Garr found the Martin and Hodgetts companies on 28 October at Red Bluffs, sixty-five miles east of Devil's Gate. The three then "started full gallop for John Hunt's camp 15 miles further."[2]

The trio reached the Hunt company in the evening. Captain Hunt was not with the company, having gone to the Platte Bridge to purchase cattle to replace the many that had died, and no one recognized the rescuers, thinking they were mountaineers. Puzzled by their reception, Young, Jones, and Garr pitched camp near the river and somewhat away from the Hunt camp. Later in the evening someone from the Hunt company wandered down to the rescuers' camp, recognized Brother Young, and "made a rush for camp, giving the word; soon [they] were literally carried in and a special tent was pitched for [their] use."[3] The Hunt Journal entry for 28 October reads, "The weather continues cold. Brothers Joseph W. Young and two other brethren [Daniel Jones and Abel Garr] arrived in camp in the evening from the Valley. This caused a general rejoicing throughout the camp, though the tidings of the snow extending westward for forty or fifty miles was not encouraging. The handcart companies had been supplied with food and clothing and the condition of the wagon companies would be reported to the Valley speedily, as the brethren traveling with teams were also getting short of provisions."

The Hunt company began moving the next day, 29 October, having successfully purchased "15 yoke of new Cattle" for thirteen hundred dollars from John Baptiste Richard at "Ft. Bridge"[4] and arrived at Devil's Gate at about 8:00 p.m. on 5 November. It was a very difficult week of travel, with very cold weather and limited food. The company spent three days at Devil's Gate, unloading the wagons and consolidating into fewer wagons. Then the company began leaving Devil's Gate at noon on 9 November, with some wagons leaving the next day.

The rescue party lead by George Grant was only the first of many groups to assist in the rescue. Speaking in general conference on 30 November 1856, Brigham Young said, "Our messengers have been traveling from here to the Platte, back and forth between Bridger, Green River and the Sweetwater; and scores of men have been riding by day and night, without having enjoyed an undisturbed night's rest during the last two months, only occasionally snatching a little sleep when sitting by the camp fire. They have been riding by day and night, hurrying to and fro and laboring with their might."[5]

2. Daniel W. Jones, *Forty Years Among the Indians* (Salt Lake City: Juvenile Instructor Office, 1890), 65.
3. Jones, 67.
4. Thomas Foster Thomas Jr. to Brigham Young, 31 October 1856, CHL, CR 1234 1_b0003_v0003.
5. *Deseret News*, 10 December 1856; see appendix 5 for text of complete speech.

When we arrived at Devil's Gate it was bitter cold.[34] We left lots of our things there. There were two or three log houses there, and we left our wagon there and joined teams with a man by the name of James Farmer. He had a sister Mary [who had] frozen to death.[35] We stayed there two or three days. While there an ox fell on the ice, and the brethren killed it, and the beef was given out to the camp. We made soup of it. My brother James ate a hearty supper and was as well as he ever was when he went to bed. In the morning he was dead.[36]

I got my feet frozen and lost all of my toes. My brother Edwin got his feet frozen bad. My sister Carrie's feet [were] frozen.[37] It was nothing but snow. We could not drive the pegs in for our tents. Father would clean a place for our tents and put snow around to keep

34. Robert T. Burton of the rescue company recorded the following on 6 November 1856 at Devil's Gate: "Colder than ever. Thermometer 11 degrees below zero. . . . None of the companies moved, so cold the people could not travel."
35. In the Larsen manuscript this name is rendered as Barman, but on close examination of the holograph it appears to be Farmer. James Morris Farmer (age thirty-nine) and his wife, Mary Ann Biddie Farmer (age twenty-six), together with three daughters (ages twelve, ten, and seven) and James' sister, Mary Ann (or Mary Jane) Farmer (age twenty-six), were members of the Hunt company. However, none of the Farmer family died on the trek. Some lists include James Barman and his sister May (or Mary) as members of the Hunt company, but the only source for this appears to be the transcripts of Mary's autobiography. They do not appear in the Pioneer Travel database of company members. See Riverton Wyoming Stake, *Remember: The Willie and Martin Handcart Companies and Their Rescuers—Past and Present* (Salt Lake City: Publishers Press, 1997), E-24.
36. According to Mary's granddaughters, "Edwin, 11, slept with his four-year-old brother, Jimmy. Edwin tried to wake him in the morning, crying, 'Jimmy, wake up! Jimmy you are so cold, please wake up. Oh Jimmy!' but Jimmy had died in the night. . . . Edwin had horrible dreams of that terrible night his entire life. He would cry out in the night, 'Jimmy! Jimmy!' His wife would wake him and say, 'It's OK, we're home, all is well.'" Document in possession of author.
37. Although Mary does not mention it here, Harriet may have also suffered frozen toes. One family record states that Mary, Caroline, and Harriet all lost toes to gangrene. Jerry Garret, "Penfold—Goble Family History" (typewritten manuscript dated 22 June 1992, in possession of the author), 5.

Devil's Gate

The Hunt Journal on 5 November 1856 reads as follows:

> The company started at 11 o'clock a.m., passed Independence Rock at 2 p.m. and arrived at the log house at Devil's Gate at 8 p.m. Here Brother Hodgetts' company [was] encamped. [The Martin company had moved to Martin's Cove the day before.] Brother [George D.] Grant and other brethren from the Valley were stopping here to give the emigrating Saints instructions in regard to their further journeyings to the Valley. A meeting was called which was addressed by Brothers Grant, Cyrus H. Wheelock and Robert T. Burton. Brother Grant informed the emigrants that they would have to leave their goods at this place (until they could be sent for), such as stoves, boxes of tools, spare clothing, etc., and only take along sufficient clothing to keep them warm [and] their bedding. He wanted four or five wagons and teams to assist the handcart companies and he expected them to take only about half the number of wagons along. All present expressed their willingness to do whatever was expected of them. The distance traveled during that day was 12 miles.

The "log house" referred to the abandoned Fort Seminoe. Charles Lajuenesse built a fort near Devil's Gate in 1852 but abandoned the fort in the fall of 1855. While the Hunt Journal uses the singular "log cabin," Mary and others refer to more than one cabin. Patience Loader recalled that at least one structure was partially torn down for firewood:

> "Brother George Grant . . . told us all to stand back, for he was going to knock down one of those log huts to make fires for us. He said, 'You are not going to freeze tonight.' . . . He raised his ax and with one blow knocked in the whole front of the building, took each log and split it in four pieces, and gave each family one piece."[1]

Josiah Rogerson remembered "eight or ten log cabins."[2]

George D. Grant, captain of the rescue party, left twenty men—seventeen from the wagon companies and three rescuers—at Fort Seminoe to guard the baggage left behind by the emigrants. The twenty-man guard, including thirteen from the Hunt company, had just twenty days of rations to last them the winter and were reduced to eating old moccasins and even an old buffalo hide rug. "There was not money enough on earth to have hired me to stay," recalled Dan Jones. "I had left home for only a few days and was not prepared to remain so long away; but I remembered my assertion that any of us would stay if called upon. I could not back out."[3]

---

1. Archer, 84.
2. Josiah Rogerson, "Martin's Handcart Company, 1856," *Salt Lake Herald-Republican*, 24 November 1907.
3. Jones, 72.

it down.³⁸ We were short of flour, but father was a good shot.³⁹ They called him the hunter of the camp, so that helped us out. We could not get enough flour for bread as we got only a quarter of a pound per head per day, so we would make it like thin gruel. We called it "skilly."⁴⁰

Well, there were four companies on the plains.⁴¹ We did not know what would become of us, when one night a man came to our camp telling us there would be plenty of flour in the morning for Bro. Brigham had sent men and teams to help us. There was rejoicing that night. Some sang, some danced, some cried. Well, he was a living Santy Claus. I have forgotten his name, but never will I forget how he looked. He was covered with the frost, and his beard was long and all frost.⁴²

38. This is corroborated by Elizabeth Stewart: "The ground was frozen so hard they could not drive the tent pins, so they had to raise the tent poles and stretch out the flaps and bank them down with snow." Stewart, https://history.churchofjesuschrist.org/overlandtravel/sources/12707365103905597270-eng/stewart-elizabeth-white-autobiography-in-workman-mary-ellen-b-comp-ancestors-of-isaac-mitton-stewart-and-elizabeth-white-1978?firstName=Elizabeth&surname=White.
39. The company roster shows that William brought two shotguns and a rifle on the journey. See "John A. Hunt Company Report, 1856," CHL, CR 1234 5, https://catalog.lds.org/assets/3961bddb-69ef-4a08-a650-dfc113cd5a92/0/1.
40. "Skilly" was a British term for a weak broth, typically made with a little oatmeal. It was often served on ships and was standard fare for prisoners on ships in the nineteenth century.
41. The Willie company arrived in Salt Lake City on 9 November 1856, the same day the other companies began moving out from Devil's Gate. After emptying the wagons at Fort Seminoe, most of the handcarts were left behind and the essential supplies were transferred to wagons. From Devil's Gate to South Pass, over nine hundred pioneers were strung out in a line that was often several miles long.
42. At this point, Mary's holograph shows this addition in pencil: "His name was Eph Hanks." Although the company had been with members of the rescue party since 28 October, food was scarce and no one knew when they would find additional relief wagons.

Ephraim Hanks and Arza Hinckley

The story of Ephraim Hanks's participation in the rescue was first published in the *Contributor* in March 1893 and was written by Andrew Jenson. Jenson begins his narrative with this paragraph: "In June, 1891, when visiting the Sevier Stake of Zion in the interest of Church history, I became acquainted with Elder Ephraim K. Hanks, who resides in Pleasant Creek, (in the Blue Valley Ward), now in Wayne County, Utah. He related to me the following."[1] He then writes, in Hanks's voice, a detailed account of Hanks's experience with the Martin company.

An additional account is given by Luna Ardell Hinckley Paul, daughter of Arza Erastus Hinckley, and is recorded by her son, Earl S. Paul.[2] Both this account and Jenson's account were written long after the events had taken place, and both are based on recollections of what was told to them—in Jenson's case by Hanks himself; in Paul's case by the daughter of Arza Hinckley. Hinckley gives a brief firsthand account of the events in a reminiscence written around 1874:

> I went out and met the first hand cart company 400 miles and traveled in with them. Started out again to see the last hand carts. 2 weeks later as Pres. B. Young carriage went out as far as Big Canyon Creek [East Canyon] where on the following he took very sick and as soon as he was able to ride returned home. 2 weeks later I started again to meet the last Co. of carts in co[mpany] with Dan Johnson each with 4 mules loads of provision and medesons [medicine] for the sick. When at Bridger Ft. there came a blizzard which detained us a few days. The first night out from there one of the mules died in D. J [Dan Johnson's] team. Next day we met 2 companies on their way home that had been out to near the Pacific Springs and could not hear any thing of the h[and] carts but after my making some persuasions they went on to camp one way and waited there until they heard of the carts then went after them. Dan and I went on to Green River where a team over took us when they took D. J. load and he went back to Bridger as his was large mules of Pres. Young and was not used, [to] being out doors at night. We met the handcart folks at Ice Springs on Sweet Water River, from there in to Salt Lake City. Eph Hanks, one of my battalion chums spent much of our time while in camp in administering to the sick. Ephraim was a man of great faith.[3]

---

1. Andrew Jenson, "The Belated Emigration of 1856," *Contributor*, March 1893.
2. "The Handcart Companies of 1856 and Arza Erastus Hinckley," CHL, M273.41 P324 1980.
3. Arza E. Hinckley, Autobiography (1874), 2, CHL, MS 10863.

Sometime after the initial rescue party left on 7 October, probably about 27 October, Ephraim Hanks set out to help in the rescue in response to a call by Heber C. Kimball to send additional assistance to the emigrants. He was apparently not part of a formal rescue party but may have met up with others on the trail. He traveled as far east as Pacific Springs, where he encountered severe weather but found no sign of the emigrant companies.

Arza Hinckley was working as a teamster for Brigham Young in 1856. In late July of that year, Arza left Salt Lake as part of the resupply party that traveled four hundred miles east to deliver food to the first handcart company. He then stayed with the company, pulling a handcart much of the way and letting emigrants ride in his wagon. He had been back in the valley only about two weeks when Brigham Young asked Arza to drive him east to help in the rescue of the Willie and Martin companies. They traveled only as far as Big Canyon Creek (East Canyon), where Brigham became very ill and they returned to the city. A few days later, Arza Hinckley and Dan Johnson left with two wagons of supplies pulled by Brigham Young's mules and headed east.

According to Paul's account, Arza and Hanks traveled together from Green River and on 10 November made camp early in the day, presumably to rest the mules. Arza stayed with the wagons and teams, and Ephraim went to hunt a buffalo. Ephraim succeeded in shooting a buffalo, skinning it, and loading his packhorse with meat, a remarkable feat. It was about an hour before sunset when he saw a long black line to the east and realized it was probably the handcart company. He rode to the company as they were setting up camp for the evening and distributed the meat, to the great joy of the emigrants. Paul states that Ephraim returned to Arza that night, and the two of them drove their provision wagons to the emigrant camp early the next morning.

Although some members of the Grant rescue party were traveling with the emigrants at this time, provisions were very scarce. There were nearly a thousand emigrants in the three companies (Martin, Hodgetts, and Hunt) and only a few rescue party members with limited supplies at this point of journey. The members of the rescue party had been stretched to their limits and were in jeopardy along with the emigrants. Food was being rationed until additional relief wagons could reach the emigrants, but the location of the relief wagons was unknown. Hanks's buffalo meat was cause for genuine rejoicing, as was the news that additional supply wagons were nearby.

Hanks and Hinckley both stayed with the emigrants during the remainder of the journey. Hanks used his considerable wilderness medical skills to help the emigrants: "Many such I washed with water and castile soap, until the frozen parts would fall off, after which I would sever the shreds of flesh from the remaining portions of the limbs with my scissors."[4]

---

4. Jenson, 204–5.

Present-day Wyoming wilderness. The wagon companies passed through treacherous terrain to reach the Salt Lake Valley. Courtesy of Jim Black/Pixabay.

Elizabeth Sermon of the Martin company corroborates this primitive surgery: "I had to take a portion of poor Robert's feet off which pierced my very soul. I had to sever the leaders with a pair of scissors. Little did I think when I bought them in old England that they would be used for such a purpose."[5]

Years later, in a letter to Wilford Woodruff, Hinckley suggested that Hanks might be a good candidate to serve with him in his mission among the American Indians in Arizona: "I believe . . . with such a man as Ephraim Hanks, if we were as well united in faith and feelings as we were when we were out to meet the [Martin] handcart company, that we would be willing to keep going south" and preach to the remaining Indian tribes.[6]

---

5. Elizabeth Whittear Sermon Camm, *Reminiscences*, in Joel Edward Ricks, Cache Valley Historical Material (ca. 1955), excerpts at https://history.churchofjesuschrist.org/overlandtravel/.
6. Arza Hinckley to Wilford Woodruff, 15 January 1883, in Joel Hinckley Bowen, *Arza Erastus Hinckley, 1826–1901* (n.p., repr. 1999 by Gene and Mary Kay Roskelley Sorensen with additions by Patra Anne Hepworth), copy in possession of author.

Arrival of the Hunt Company

Most members of the Martin company arrived in Salt Lake on 30 November, but the wagon companies traveled more slowly since they had ox teams rather than horses. They stayed some days at Fort Bridger, where the animals could rest and feed and where some of the weakest Saints could gain strength before the last difficult leg of the journey.

On 3 December 1856 the *Deseret News* contained the following notice:

> CAPS. HODGETTS AND HUNT'S COMPANIES.—A few have been brought in from the only companies still back, but the remainder are unable to come in without assistance. For this reason some 60 horse and mule teams, mostly with two spans to a wagon, left this city on the 2nd inst. with a supply of provisions and forage expected to be amply sufficient for all wants, as the out-going wagons will load back with persons, and will probably be able to bring in all who can endure the journey, or are not needed to help take care of animals that may have to be left at Forts Bridger and Supply until spring.[1]

The mentioned teams and wagons that left on 2 December were the last rescue group to leave the Salt Lake Valley and departed nearly two months after the first rescue company had left.

The *Mormon*, a Church newspaper in New York City, in a story published on 21 February 1857, quoted from a letter written by Brigham Young that was dated 6 December 1856:

> "The last of our hand-cart emigration arrived on last Sunday, the 30th ult. The so-called independent company [that is, independent of the PEF], with ox trains, have not arrived; but are supposed to be at Bridger's Fort; sufficient assistance has gone to their relief to bring them all safely into the city. The weather has been steadily cold since the first of November, and considerable snow south and in the mountains, but not much in the valley, or on the line of travel as far east as the pass, except on the mountains, where it has been somewhat difficult to keep the roads open."[2]

The final entry in the Hunt Journal is dated Monday, 15 December 1856: "The remainder of the saints arrived in Great Salt Lake City today, the emigration being now completed."[3]

---

1. *Deseret News*, 3 December 1856.
2. *Mormon* 3, no. 1 (21 February 1857), https://archive.org/details/TheMormom18551857/page/n413/mode/2up.
3. Hunt Journal, 15 December 1856.

We traveled faster now that we had horse teams,⁴³ and we arrived in Salt Lake City at 9 o'clock at night the 11th of December 1856.⁴⁴ Three out of four that were living were frozen. My mother was dead in the wagon.⁴⁵

Bishop Hardy⁴⁶ had us taken to a house in his ward, and the brethren and the sisters fetched us plenty of food. We had to be careful and not eat too much as it might kill us as we were so hungry.

43. The Larsen manuscript includes these sentences inserted at this point: "My mother had never got well; she lingered until 11 December, the day we arrived in Salt Lake City, 1856. She died between the Little and Big Mountain[s]. She was buried in the Salt Lake City Cemetery. She was 43 years old. She and her baby lost their lives gathering to Zion in such a late season of the year. My sister was buried at the last crossing of the Sweetwater."

44. The Hunt Journal notes on 11 December, "The snow was 6 to 10 inches deep in G. S. L. City. Some teams arrived from Ft. Bridger." On 12 December it notes, "The snow was 10 to 12 inches deep in G. S. L. City and it was still snowing." The last of the wagon companies arrived in Salt Lake on 15 December 1856.

45. In a letter to Samuel S. Jones dated 18 October 1908, Mary wrote, "Our mother never got well. She lingered for 11 weeks and died the 11 December 1856, between the Big and Little Mountain[s] about 4 o'clock in the afternoon. She was buried in the City Cemetery. I rode in the same bed with my dead mother till 9 o'clock that night." See appendix 2.

46. Leonard Wilford Hardy, age fifty-five, was the police chief of Salt Lake City and bishop of the Twelfth Ward. A native of Massachusetts, he was baptized at age twenty-six by Orson Hyde on 2 December 1832 and accompanied Wilford Woodruff on a mission to Liverpool in 1845, laboring in Manchester and presiding over the Preston Conference. He arrived in Utah on 14 October 1850 in the Wilford Woodruff company. On 17 December 1856, the *Deseret News* published this report: "Bishop L. W. Hardy reports the new arrivals to be in fine spirits, notwithstanding their late hardships; and those who so liberally turned out to their relief report themselves ready to start out again, were it necessary. But few in the two rear companies were frosted, and of those only one or two severely. Bishop Hardy at once threw open his doors to the family in which were the ones most severely frosted, and under his judicious nursing, without amputation, they are rapidly recovering; though the one most frosted will, perhaps, be somewhat crippled in her feet."

The next day the bishop came and brought a doctor. His name was Williams.[47] He amputated our feet. The sisters were dressing mother for her grave. My poor father walked in the room where mother was, then back to us. He could not shed a tear. When our feet were fine they packed us in to see our mother for the last time. Oh, how did we stand it? That afternoon she was buried.[48]

• • •

47. This was likely Ezra Granger Williams, who was a physician and surgeon in Salt Lake City at the time. The son of Frederick G. Williams (who served as a counselor to Joseph Smith in the First Presidency), Ezra was born on 17 November 1823. He was baptized by Joseph Smith in the Chagrin River in Kirtland and confirmed by Hyrum Smith in Hyrum's home on 14 April 1832. He arrived in 1849 in Salt Lake City, where he practiced medicine until 1860. He later moved to Ogden.

48. The Larsen manuscript replaces this paragraph with the following: "Early next morning Bro. Brigham Young and a doctor came. The doctor's name was Williams. When Bro. Young came in he shook hands with us all. When he saw our condition, our feet frozen and our mother dead, tears rolled down his cheeks.

"The doctor wanted to cut my feet off at the ankles. But Pres. Young said no just cut off the toes and I promise you, you will never have to take them off any farther. The pieces of bone that must come out will work out through the skin themselves.

"The doctor amputated my toes using a saw and a butcher knife. The sisters were dressing mother for her grave. My poor father walked in the room where mother was, then back to us. He could not shed a tear. When our feet were fixed they packed us in to see our mother for the last time. Oh, how did we stand it? That afternoon she was buried."

Caroline "Carrie" Goble Bowers and Mary Goble Pay.

It is now October 1906.⁴⁹ Fifty years ago we left our homes over the sea for Utah. Quite a few of us that are left have been to Salt Lake City to celebrate our Jubilee.⁵⁰ We met in the 14th Ward assembly hall.⁵¹ We held three meetings. President Joseph F. Smith and the Relief Society furnished us a banquet. We had a very good time. I stayed with Anna Pay Kimball.⁵² We met the captain of our company, Brother John Hunt, [and] met some of the people that came in our company. We were happy to see one another and talk of the times that are gone.

My sister Carrie and her husband went up to the city with us. Her husband came in Captain Ellsworth's handcart company.⁵³ We went to conference [for] two days and then went to the cemetery to find my mother's grave. It was in Lot 2, plot C. It was the first time

---

49. The holograph says "1896," but this was crossed out, and "1906" had been written above it.
50. The jubilee was organized by the Handcart Veterans Association and held 3–5 October 1906. It received extensive newspaper coverage that included stories from many of the pioneers. It concluded with a Friday night meeting in the Assembly Hall on Temple Square, where Utah governor John Cutler addressed the participants. The Jubilee chairman was Samuel Stephen Jones, who was nineteen when he emigrated with the Martin company. Mary traveled from Nephi to attend the Jubilee. See Handcart Veterans Association scrapbook, 1906–1914, CHL MS 11378.
51. The Fourteenth Ward building was located at 142 West 200 North in Salt Lake City.
52. Anna Sinclair Pay Kimball was Mary's daughter-in-law. Anna Sinclair was born in Moroni, Utah, on 14 October 1864 and married George Pay, Mary and Richard's second child, in 1883. George died in 1894, one year after Richard's death. Anna then married Charles Spaulding Kimball, a son of Heber C. Kimball, in 1900. Charles died in 1925, leaving Anna widowed again. Anna died at eighty-four as the result of an automobile accident in 1949. She was buried next to George Pay in the Vine Bluff Cemetery in Nephi.
53. On 19 January 1867, Carrie married Jacob Bowers, who was ten when he walked across the plains as part of the Edmund Ellsworth handcart company. He arrived in Salt Lake on 26 September 1856, just two days after little Edith Goble was born on the trail in Nebraska.

Mary Goble Pay with children and grandchildren.

I had seen it, for when she was buried our feet were so bad [that] we could not go to the funeral, and [then] the move came, and we moved south to Nephi.

No one knows how I felt as we stood there by her grave. There were Alma, his wife, myself, and Ethel, one of George's daughters. There were three generations.[54] Our mother was a martyr for the truth. I thought of her words, "Polly, I want to go to Zion while my children are small, so they can be raised in the Gospel of Christ, for I know this is the true Church."

Now there are 31 grandchildren [and] 26 great-grandchildren living, and 15 are dead. There are three of us living—my brother, sister, and myself. . . . I think my mother has her wish. My brother and three of my sons have [ful]filled missions,[55] and some of her grandsons and [grand]daughters are workers in the Church. They are all members of the Church. I now have six sons and one daughter living, four sons are married, and I have eleven grandchildren. I am proud of them all. I am the mother of thirteen children, ten sons and three daughters. My brother Edwin is the father of fifteen sons and daughters. My sister Carrie is the mother of nine—five sons and four daughters. My sister Harriet is [also] the mother of nine—seven sons and two daughters. [56]

• • •

---

54. The three generations were Mary Goble Pay, her son David Alma Pay (born 25 May 1873), and granddaughter Ethel Pay (born 4 October 1862, daughter of George Edwin Pay).
55. Mary's brother, Edwin, served in Liverpool (1890–91). Her three missionary sons were Edward (England, 1898–?), Jesse (Central States, 1898–1900; and Southern States, 1925–26), and LeRoy (Southern States, 1906–8). While in England, Edward baptized Mary's aunt, Emma Penfold Simmonds, and at least one of Mary's cousins (Emma's daughter), Ada. Ada immigrated to Utah in 1909, crossing the country by train in four days. She lived with Mary in Nephi until she married in 1912. See Jerry Garrett, "Penfold—Goble Family History" (typewritten manuscript dated 22 June 1992), 6, https://www.familysearch.org/tree/person/memories/KWJ8-R57).
56. At the date of this entry, the four Goble children who survived the trek had forty-six children between them.

Nephi, Oct. 1908. Have been to our Handcart Reunion.[57] I met quite a few old friends. Went to conference. My brother and I went to see my mother's grave. They had renumbered them. It is plot F, Lot 8 or 12.[58] We will have it fixed [and] leveled and [have] grass sown on it.

• • •

Oct. 21, 1909. Went to Sunday School and was asked to relate incidents of our journey across the plains. I told them we had the first snow storm the 22nd of September, 1856.[59] There were fifteen who died through crossing the River Platte.[60] Sister McPherson[61] sat by me. She said, "My mother was the fifteenth one that died." They were laid side by side and a little dirt [was] thrown over them.[62]

57. After the success of the reunion in 1906, the Handcart Veterans Association voted to do annual reunions.
58. Now Plot F, Section F, 11/12. The marker is approximately forty feet east of the cemetery's Main Street, between 310 North and 330 North.
59. The Hunt Journal notes that the weather on 23 September 1856 was "cold and frosty" but makes no mention of a storm on the 22nd; the first snowstorm was the night of 19 October.
60. As noted previously, there are various accounts regarding the number of emigrants who died.
61. Jane Ann Ollerton McPherson was sixteen when she emigrated with her family. They sailed on the *Horizon* and were part of the Martin company. Both of her parents died on the journey. She moved to Nephi, where she met and married James Ramsey McPhereson. She died in 1933 at the age of ninety-two and is buried in the same cemetery as Mary Goble and Richard Pay. Jane Ann's sister, Alice Ollerton, died the day after the family reached the Salt Lake Valley; she is buried in the Salt Lake City Cemetery next to Mary Penfold Goble. Jane Ann's daughter Bertha McPherson wrote a short biographical sketch of her mother in 1950 in which she says, "Several times I asked mother to give me some information so that I could write a sketch of her life, but she always answered by saying, 'My life has been very uneventful.'" Bertha McPherson, "Jane Ann Ollerton McPherson" (unpublished manuscript), https://www.familysearch.org/tree/person/memories/KWJW-455.
62. On 15 April 1933, Harry Mills, a rancher near Casper, Wyoming, chanced upon some human bones in a small gulch near the North Platte River. Excavations

• • •

November. I have been to our reunion. I met Bro. Langley Bailey.[63] Had a good time. Told of incidents of our trip over the plains. It made us feel bad—it brought it all up again. Is it wise for our children to see what their parents passed through for the Gospel? Yes.

---

over the following days revealed nine skeletons: five men, three women, and an infant. One of the skeletons was in a sitting position, suggesting that he had frozen. These may have been members of the Martin company. The remains were reinterred in Potters Field in the Highland Cemetery in Casper. The find was reported in the *Casper Tribune Herald* on 16 April 1933 and 17 April 1933 and discussed in the *Wyoming Trails Newsletter* 17, no. 3 (March 2005). Information courtesy of R. Scott Lorimer.

63. Langley Bailey was a member of the Martin company, one of the four sons of John and Jane Bailey. Langley was eighteen during the trek but weighed only sixty pounds upon arriving in the valley. The family settled in Nephi, where Langley became a patriarch years later. He spoke at the funeral of Mary Goble Pay in 1913. His great-granddaughter Margaret Dyreng Nadauld served as Young Women General President from 1997 to 2002 and spoke of her great-grandfather in the general Young Women meeting on 27 March 1999.

Epilogue

After arriving in the Salt Lake Valley on 11 December 1856, Mary and her family remained for a week in Salt Lake. "One afternoon," she wrote, "there came a knock at the door. It was uncle John Wood. When he met father he said, 'I know it all, Bill.' Both of them cried. Oh, I was glad to see my father cry." The Gobles went to Farmington, where they stayed with the Woods until the following April. Mary's widowed father, William Goble, met Susannah Patching, a member of the Martin company, the evening he arrived in Farmington, and the two were married the next day. Mary says simply, "My father remarried."[1]

---

1. Susannah Patching was forty-nine and had never been married; William was a thirty-nine-year-old widower with four living children and four deceased children. William and Susannah appear in the 1860 census in Nephi as husband and wife and were sealed in the Endowment House on 8 December 1865.

Because of the condition of her feet, Mary could not get her shoes on until June. In July she went to live with a Dr. Wiseman, who told her that she had gangrene in her feet and that they would have to be removed at the ankle. Relying on the promise of Brigham Young that she would never have to have any more of her feet cut off, she refused. Mary only says that an old woman came to the house one day and applied a poultice that healed her feet, to the amazement of the doctor. Mary went through a painful but successful rehabilitation to learn how to walk again, adding, "I have never had to have any more taken from them. The promise of Brigham Young has been fulfilled and the pieces of toe bone have worked out."[2]

In the spring of 1858, William and his family moved south to Nephi, where his sister, Mary Ann, and her husband, Thomas Carter, had settled five years earlier. Mary stayed at Spanish Fork for a year before going on to Nephi in the spring of 1859. In Nephi she stayed with her aunt and uncle. On 26 June 1859, she married Richard Pay. She was sixteen, and he was thirty-seven.

Richard and Sarah, his first wife, both of whom had joined the Church in Dover, Kent, England, had sailed from Liverpool on the *Horizon* with the Gobles. Richard is listed on the ship register as a shoemaker. Both the Gobles and the Pays were members of the Hunt company. William Goble helped Richard bury an infant daughter

---

William was sealed to Mary Penfold on the same day. Susannah died 29 August 1892 and is buried next to William in Vine Bluff Cemetery in Nephi, Utah. A widower again at age seventy-five, William married Mary Ann Ewers Fowkes, the widow of James Fowkes. Mary Ann died on 17 February 1898, and William followed her in death about two weeks later, 9 March 1898. Their deaths were noted in an obituary in the *Salt Lake Herald* on 10 March 1898 under the headline "Passing of the Pioneers: William Goble of Nephi Quickly Follows His Wife to the Grave."

2. This information appears in the Larsen manuscript but is not included in Mary's holograph. Dr. John Wiseman and his wife Mary Ann were members of the Hunt company. He is listed in the roster as a surgeon, and they are the only Wisemans who appear in emigration records before 1857. The Wisemans' two sons, ages two and seven, died during the journey. They may have taken Mary in partly to provide some companionship for Mary Ann Wiseman.

Mary Goble Pay and Richard Pay.

Pay Cabin in Leamington.

at Chimney Rock, and Richard helped William bury little Edith in Wyoming. Richard's wife, Sarah, died at Fort Bridger, leaving him alone. In the spring of 1857, Richard—who had had sufficient means to purchase passage to America for his family and outfit an ox team in 1856—walked with all his earthly belongings tied up in a handkerchief from Salt Lake City to Nephi.

Of their early years together, Mary says simply, "When I was married it was very hard times." They were refugees in a foreign land, scraping out an existence by growing a few crops in an environment that could not have been more different from England's green and pleasant land. And like so many others, Mary and Richard had left loved ones buried in graves they would never visit.

Mary eventually bore thirteen children, three of whom died in infancy. She and Richard were sealed in the Endowment House in Salt Lake City on 8 December 1865; that same day, she was sealed to her father and her deceased mother.[3] The family lived in Nephi for

---

3. As noted earlier, William Goble was sealed to Mary Penfold and Susannah Patching on this same date.

Pay cabin at This is the Place Heritage Park, 2019, with descendants of Mary Goble Pay.

twenty-two years, then moved to nearby Leamington, Utah, where Richard built a little log house on 160 acres that they homesteaded. The 1880 census lists Richard as a shepherd. Mary and Richard lived with seven of their children (three had died in infancy and three would be born later) in that little cabin before building a small two-story home on the farm. The cabin was moved to This Is The Place Heritage Park in 2001.

Richard died 18 April 1893 at age seventy-one, leaving forty-nine-year-old Mary with seven children still at home (two of whom had been born in the little cabin in Leamington). The next year her oldest living son, George, died, leaving a wife and five children. Her daughter Sarah died the following year at age fourteen. Mary then returned to Nephi, where she supported the family by working as a practical nurse.

Mary reported that her deceased husband came to visit her on several occasions in dreams or visions. On 14 September 1913, she told her daughter Ettie, with whom she was living, that Richard had visited her again during the night and had everything ready for her to come and be with him. She died quietly the next morning with her children gathered around her. She was seventy years old and was buried in the Vine Bluff Cemetery in Nephi next to her husband.

• • •

On 11 December 2006, more than 250 descendants of Mary Goble and Richard Pay—all active members of The Church of Jesus Christ of Latter-day Saints—gathered in the Social Hall at This Is The Place Heritage Park to mark the 150th anniversary of Mary's arrival into the valley. It was a cold winter night, but all were dressed in warm coats, warm hats, and warm gloves. They arrived in warm cars, met in a warm building, and returned to warm homes.

Mary Goble Pay.

All glory to the Pioneers! God bless their memory,
their works, their children, forever!

—Bryant S. Hinckley, 1953

Appendix 1
Comparison of Holograph, Larsen Manuscript, Bowers Transcript, and Pay Transcript

HOLOGRAPH: Transcription of Holograph scanned from ledger book in possession of Bowers family; organized into sentences with punctuation added.

LARSEN: Transcription of handwritten record in notebook of Vera Pay Larsen.

PAY: "Life of Mary Goble Pay" (autobiography from Pay family).

BOWERS: "Mary Goble Pay Family History" (autobiography from Bowers family).

Note: The texts have been divided into numbered blocks for ease of reference.

#	Holograph	Larsen	Pay	Bowers
1	Nephi City, Feb 1903			
2	I Mary Goble was born in Brighton Sussex england June the 2 1843. My Father was William Goble son of William and Harriet Johnson Goble. My mother was the Daughter of John and sarah Penfold.	¶ I, Mary Goble was born in Brighton, Sussex, England June 2, 1843. My father was William Goble, son of William and Harriet Johnson Goble. My mother was the daughter of John and Sarah Penfold.	¶ I, Mary Goble was born in Brighton, Sussex, England June 2, 1843. My father was William Goble, son of William and Harriet Johnson Goble. My mother was the daughter of John and Sarah Penfold.	¶ I Mary Goble was born in Brighton Sussex England 2 June 1843. My father William Goble was son of William and Harriet Johnson Goble. My mother was the daughter of John and Sarah Penfold.
3	My Childhood day was spent the same as most Children.	¶ My childhood days were spent the same as most children.	¶ My childhood days were spent the same as most children.	My childhood days were spent the same as most children.
4	When i was in my 12 year my parents Joined the Latterday saints.	When I was in my twelfth year, my parents joined the Latter-Day-Saints.	When I was in my twelfth year, my parents joined the Latter-Day-Saints.	When I was in my twelfth year, my parents joined the Latter-Day Saints church.
5	on Nov the 5 i was baptised.	On November 5th I was baptized.	On November 5th I was baptized.	On November 5th I was baptized.
6	The following may we started for utah. We Left our home may the 19, 1856.	The following May we started for Utah. We left our home May 19, 1856.	The following May we started for Utah. We left our home May 19, 1856.	The following May we started for Utah. We left our home May 19, 1856.
7	We came to London the first day the next day came to Liverpool and went on Board the ship Horizon that eve[n]ing.	We came to London the first day, the next day came to Liverpool and went on board the ship, Horizon, that evening	We came to London the first day, the next day came to Liverpool and went on board the ship, Horizon, that evening	We came to London the first day, the next day went to Liverpool and went on board the ship, Horizon that evening.

#	Holograph	Larsen	Pay	Bowers
8	It was sailing vessel. There were nearly 9 hundred souls on board.	¶ It was a sailing Vessel and there were nearly nine hundred souls on board.	¶ It was a sailing Vessel and there were nearly nine hundred souls on board.	Its was a sailing Vessel and there were nearly nine hundred souls on board.
9	We sailed on the 25. The pilot ship came and tug us out into the open sea.	We sailed on the 25th. The pilot ship came and tugged us out into the open sea.	We sailed on the 25th. The pilot ship came and tugged us out into the open sea.	We sailed on the 25th. The pilot ship came and tugged us out into the open sea.
10	I well Remmember how we watched old england fade from sight. We sang farewell our native Land farewell.	¶ I well remember how we watched old England fade from sight. We Sang "Farewell our Native land Farewell."	¶ I well remember how we watched old England fade from sight. We Sang "Farewell our Native land Farewell."	¶ I well remember how we watched old England fade from sight. We Sang "Farewell Our Native land Farewell."
11	While we were in the River the Crew mutin[i]ed but they where [were] put Ashore and another crew came on Board. They were a good set of men.	¶ While we were in the river the crew mutinied but they were put ashore and another crew came on board. They were a good set of men.	¶ While we were in the river the crew mutinied but they were put ashore and another crew came on board. They were a good set of men.	While we were in the river the crew mutinied but they were put ashore and another crew came on board. They were a good set of men.
12	When we were a few days out a Large shark follwd the vessel. There was one of the saints died. He was buried in the sea. We never saw the shark any more.	¶ When we were a few days out, a large shark followed the vessel. One of the saints died and he was buried at sea. We never saw the shark anymore.	¶ When we were a few days out, a large shark followed the vessel. One of the saints died and he was buried at sea. We never saw the shark anymore.	¶ When we were a few days out, a large shark followed our vessel. One of the saints died and he was buried at sea. We never saw the shark anymore.

#	Holograph	Larsen	Pay	Bowers
13	After we got over our sea sickness we had a nice time. We would play games sing songs of Zion. We held meetings and the time passed happily.	¶ After we got over our seasickness we had a nice time. We would play games, and sing songs of zion. We held meetings and the time passed happily.	¶ After we got over our seasickness we had a nice time. We would play games, and sing songs of zion. We held meetings and the time passed happily.	¶ After we got over our seasickness we had a nice time. We would play games and sing song of Zion. We held meetings and the time passed happily.
14	When we where [were] sailing through the Banks of New foundland we where [were] in a dense fog for several days, the sailors where [were] kept night and Day Ringing Bells, and blowing fog horns.	¶ When we were sailing through the banks of Newfoundland we were in a dense fog for several days. The sailors were kept night and day ringing bells and blowing fog horns.	¶ When we were sailing through the banks of Newfoundland we were in a dense fog for several days. The sailors were kept night and day ringing bells and blowing fog horns.	¶ When we were sailing through the banks of Newfoundland, we were in a dense fog for several days. The sailors were kept night and day ringing bells and blowing fog horn.
15	One day i was on deck with my father when i saw Like a mountain of ice in the sea close to the ship.	¶ One day I was on deck with my father when I saw a mountain of ice in the sea close to the ship.	¶ One day I was on deck with my father when I saw a mountain of ice in the sea close to the ship.	One day I was on deck with my father, when I saw a mountain of ice in the sea close to the ship.
16	I said Look father Look. He whent as white as a ghost and said, oh my Girl	I said, "Look, father look". He went white as a ghost and said, "Oh, my girl".	I said, "Look, father look". He went white as a ghost and said, "Oh, my girl".	I said, Look father, Look! He went pale as a ghost and said, Oh my girl.
17	At that moment the fog parted. The sun shone Bright till the ship was out of danger when the fog closed on us again.	At that moment the fog parted the sun shone bright till the ship was out of danger when the fog closed on us again.	At that moment the fog parted the sun shone bright till the ship was out of danger when the fog closed on us again.	At that moment the fog parted and the sun shone bright until the ship was out of danger, then the fog closed on us again.

#	Holograph	Larsen	Pay	Bowers
18	We where [were] on the sea 6 weeks when we Landed at Boston. We took train for Iowa City where we had to get our out fit for the plains. It was the end of July.	¶ We were on the sea six weeks, when we landed at Boston. We took the train for Iowa city were we had to get an outfit for the plains. It was the end of July.	¶ We were on the sea six weeks, when we landed at Boston. We took the train for Iowa city were we had to get an outfit for the plains. It was the end of July.	¶ We were on the sea six weeks then we landed at Boston. We then took the train for Iowa city were we had to get an outfit for the plains. It was the end of July.
19	On the first of Aug we started to travel with our ox teams unbroke and we did not know a thing about driving oxen.	On the first of August we started to travel with our ox teams unbroke and we did not know a thing about driving oxen.	On the first of August we started to travel with our ox teams unbroke and did not know a thing about driving oxen.	On the first of Aug. we started to travel with our ox teams unbroken and did not know a thing about driving them.
20	My father had Bought 2 yoke of oxen, 1 yoke of cows, a wagon an[d] tent.	My father had bought two yoke of oxen and one yoke of cows, a wagon and tent.	My father had bought two yoke of oxen and one yoke of cows, a wagon and tent.	My father had brought two yoke of oxens and one yoke of cows, a wagon and tent.
21	He had a wife and 6 children. There names where [were] Mary Edwin Caroline James and Fanny.	He had a wife and six children. Their names were Mary, Edwin, Caroline, Harriet, James, and Fanny.	He had a wife and six children. Their names were Mary, Edwin, Caroline, Harriet, James, and Fanny.	He had a wife and six children. Their names were Mary, Edwin, Caroline, Harriet, James, and fanny.

#	Holograph	Larsen	Pay	Bowers
22	My sister Fanny Broke out with the measels on the ship and when we were on Iowa Camp Ground there Came up a thunder storm. {Blew down our shelter and made with hand carts and some quilts. The storm came and we there in the rain thunder and litning} and she got wet and died the 19 of July 1856. She would have been 2 years on the 23 of July.	¶ My sister Fanny broke out with the measles on the ship and when we were in Iowa campground, there came up a thunder storm that blew down our shelter, made with handcarts and some quilts. The storm came and we sat there in the rain, thunder and lightning. My sister got wet and died the 19th of July 1856. She would have been 2 years old on the 23rd.	¶ My sister Fanny broke out with the measles on the ship and when we were in Iowa campground, there came up a thunder storm that blew down our shelter, made with handcarts and some quilts. The storm came and we sat there in the rain, thunder and lightning. My sister got wet and died the 19th of July 1856. She would have been 2 years old on the 23rd.	¶ My sister Fanny broke out with the measles on the ship and when we were in Iowa campground, there came a thunder storm that blew down our shelter, made with handcarts and quilts. My sister got wet and died the 19 July 1856. She would have been 2 years old on the 23.
23	The day Before we started on our journey we visited her greve [grave]. We felt awful to Leave our Little sister there.	¶ The day we started on our journey we visited her grave. We felt very bad to leave our little sister there.	¶ The day we started on our journey we visited her grave. We felt very bad to leave our little sister there.	The day we started on our journey, We visited her grave. We felt very bad to leave our little sister there.

#	Holograph	Larsen	Pay	Bowers
24	We traveled through the states till we got to Counsel Bluffs. I think that was the name. It is in wyoming. Then we started on our journey of one thousand miles over the plains. It was about the first of september.	¶ We traveled through the States until we came to Council Bluffs. Then we started on our journey of one thousand miles over the plains. ¶ It was about the 1st of September.	¶ We traveled through the States until we came to Council Bluffs. Then we started on our journey of one thousand miles over the plains. ¶ It was about the 1st of September.	¶ We traveled through the States until we came to Council bluffs. Then we started on our journey of one thousand miles over the plains. It was about the last of September.
25	We traveled from 15 to 25 miles a day. We use to stop one day in the week to wash and rested on sunday [to] hold our meetings and every morning and night we where [were] Called to prayers By the Bugle.	We traveled from 15 to 25 miles a day. We used to stop one day in the week to wash. On Sunday we would hold our meetings and rest. Every morning and night we were called to prayers by the bugle.	We traveled from 15 to 25 miles a day. We used to stop one day in the week to wash. On Sunday we would hold our meetings and rest. Every morning and night we were called to prayers by the bugle.	We would traveled about 15 to 25 miles a day. We used to stop one day in the week to wash. On Sunday we would hold our meeting and rest. Every morning and night we were called to prayers by the bugle.
26	The indians where [were] very hostile as they where [were] on the war path so our Captain J Hunt had us make a dark Camp. That was to stop and get our supper then travel a few miles and not light any fires but Camp and go to bed. The men had to travel all day and Gaurd [guard] every other night.	¶ The Indians were on the war path and were very hostile. Our Captain John Hunt had us make a dark camp. That was to stop and get our supper then travel a few miles and not light any fires but camp and go to bed. The men had to travel all day and guard every other night.	¶ The Indians were on the war path and were very hostile. Our Captain John Hunt had us make a dark camp. That was to stop and get our supper then travel a few miles and not light any fires but camp and go to bed. The men had to travel all day and guard every other night.	¶ The Indians were on the war path and very hostile. Our Captain John Hunt had us make a dark camp. That was to stop and get our supper then travel a few miles and not light any fire but camp and go to bed. The men had to travel all day and guard every other night.

#	Holograph	Larsen	Pay	Bowers
27	One night the Cattle where [were] in the corral made with the wagons when one of the Gaurds saw something Crawling along the Ground.	¶ One night the cattle were in the corral, which was made with wagons, when one of the guards saw something crawling along the ground.	¶ One night the cattle were in the corral, which was made with wagons, when one of the guards saw something crawling along the ground.	¶ One night the cattle were in the corral, which was made with the wagons. When one of the guards saw something crawling along the ground.
28	All in a moment the Cattle started. It was a noise like thunder. He shot of[f] his gun when the animal Jump[ed] up and Run. It was a indian with a Buffalo Robe. He dropped it.	All in a moment the cattle started. It was a noise like thunder. The guard shot off his gun. The animal jumped up and run. It was an Indian with a buffalo robe on.	All in a moment the cattle started. It was a noise like thunder. The guard shot off his gun. The animals jumped up and ran. It was an Indian with a buffalo robe on.	All in a moment the cattle started. It was a noise like thunder. The guard shot off his gun. The animals jumped up and ran. It was an Indian with a buffalo robe on.
29	Mother and us Children were sitting in the tent. Father was on gaurd. I tell you we thought our time was come. But father came Running to tell us not to be scared for everything was all right	Mother and we children were sitting in the tent. Father was on guard. We were surely frightened but father came running in and told us not to be afraid for everything was all right.	Mother and we children were sitting in the tent. Father was on guard. We were surely frightened but father came running in and told us not to be afraid for everything was all right.	Mother and us childrens were sitting in our tent. Father was on guard. We were surely frightened but Father came running in and told us not to be afraid for everything was all right.

#	Holograph	Larsen	Pay	Bowers
30	we traveled on till we got to the last crossing of the platt River. That was the Last walk i ever walk with my mother. We caug[ht] up with the hand cart companys that day. We watched them cross the River.	¶ We traveled on till we got to the Platt River. That was the last walk I ever had with my mother. We caught up with the Hand Cart companies that day. We watched them cross the river.	¶ We traveled on till we got to the Platt River. That was the last walk I ever had with my mother. We caught up with the Hand Cart companies that day. We watched them cross the river.	¶ We traveled on till we got to the Platt River. That was the last walk I ever had with my mother. We caught up with the handcart companies that day. We watch them cross the river.
31	There was great Lumps of ice floating down the River. It was Bitter Cold. The next morning there were 14 dead in the camp through the cold. We went Back to Camp went to prayers. They sang Come Come ye saints not toil or Labor fear.	There were great lumps of ice floating down the river. It was bitter cold. The next morning there were fourteen dead in camp through the cold. We went back to camp and went to prayers. They sang, "Come, Come, Ye Saints No Toil Nor Labor Fear".	There were great lumps of ice floating down the river. It was bitter cold. The next morning there were fourteen dead in camp through the cold. We went back to camp and went to prayers. They sang, "Come, Come, Ye Saints No Toil Nor Labor Fear".	There were great lumps of ice floating down the river. It was bitter cold. The next morning there were fourteen dead in camp from the cold. We went back to camp and said our prayers and then sang the song: Come, Come, Ye Saints No Toil Nor Labor Fear.

#	Holograph	Larsen	Pay	Bowers
32	I wonder[e]d what made my mother Cry. That night my mother took sick. The next morning my Little sister was Born. It was the 23 of sep. We name her Edith. She lived 6 weeks and died for the want of nourishment	I wondered what made my mother cry. That night my mother took sick and the next morning my little sister was born. It was the 23rd of Sept. We named her Edith and she lived six weeks and died for the want of nourishment.	I wondered what made my mother cry. That night my mother took sick and the next morning my little sister was born. It was the 23rd of Sept. We named her Edith and she lived six weeks and died for the want of nourishment.	I was wondering what made my mother cry. That night my mother took sick and the next morning my little sister was born. It was the 23rd of Sept. We name her Edith and she lived six weeks and died for want of nourishment.
33	was Buried the last crossing of the sweetwater.	See block 47 for corresponding text.	See block 47 for corresponding text.	See block 47 for corresponding text.
34	My Mother never got well. She lingered till the 11th of Dec the day we arrived in salt Lake City 1856. She died Beetween the Little and big Mountain. She was Burried in salt Lake City Cementry. Her age was 43 years. She and her Babe Lost there Life Gathering to Zion in such a Late season of the year.	See block 47 for corresponding text.	See #47	See #47

#	Holograph	Larsen	Pay	Bowers
35		¶ We had been without water for several days just drinking snow water. The captain said there was a spring of fresh water just a few miles away. It was snowing hard, but my mother begged me to go and get her a drink. Another lady went with me. We were about half way to the spring when we found an old man who had fallen in the snow. He was frozen so stiff, we could not lift him, so the lady told me where to go and she would go back to camp for help	¶ We had been without water for several days just drinking snow water. The captain said there was a spring of fresh water just a few miles away. It was snowing hard, but my mother begged me to go and get her a drink. Another lady went with me. We were about half way to the spring when we found an old man who had fallen in the snow. He was frozen so stiff, we could not lift him, so the lady told me where to go and she would go back to camp for help	¶ We had been without water for several days, just drinking snow water. The Captain said there was a spring of fresh water just a few miles away. It was snowing hard, but my mother begged me to go and get her a drink. Another lady went with me. We were about half way to the spring when we found and old man who had fallen in the snow. He was frozen so stiff, we could not lift him, so the lady told where to go for water. She would go back to camp for help.

#	Holograph	Larsen	Pay	Bowers
36		for we knew he would soon be frozen if we left him. When she had gone I began to think of the Indians and looking and looking in all directions I became confused and forgot the way I should go. I waded around in the snow up to my knees and I became lost.	for we knew he would soon be frozen if we left him. When she had gone I began to think of the Indians and looking and looking in all directions I became confused and forgot the way I should go. I waded around in the snow up to my knees and I became lost.	For we knew he would soon be frozen if we left him. When she had gone I began to think of the Indians and looks and looking in all directing. I became confused and forgot my way. I waded around in the snow up to my knees and I became lost.
37		Later when I did not return to camp the men started out after me. It was 11:00 o'clock before they found me. My feet and legs were frozen. They carried me to camp and rubbed me with snow. They put my feet in a bucket of water. The pain was terrible. The frost came out of legs and feet but not out of my toes.	Later when I did not return to camp the men started out after me. It was 11:00 o'clock before they found me. My feet and legs were frozen. They carried me to camp and rubbed me with snow. They put my feet in a bucket of water. The pain was terrible. The frost came out of legs and feet but not out of my toes.	Later when I did not return to camp the men started out to find me. It was 11:00 o'clock before they found me. My feet and legs were frozen. They carried me back to camp and rubbed me with snow. They put my feet in a bucket of water the pain was terrible. The frost came out of legs and feet but did not come out of my toes.

#	Holograph	Larsen	Pay	Bowers
38	We traveled in the snow from the last crossing of the Platte River. We had orders to not pass the hand Cart Co. We had to keep close to them so has [as] to help them if we could. We began to get short of food. Our cattle gave out. We could only travel a few miles a day.	¶ We traveled in the snow from the last crossing of the Platte River. We had orders not to pass the hand cart companies. We had to keep close to them so as to help them if we could. We began to get short of food our cattle gave out. We could only travel a few miles a day.	¶ We traveled in the snow from the last crossing of the Platte River. We had orders not to pass the hand cart companies. We had to keep close to them so as to help them if we could. We began to get short of food and our cattle gave out. We could only travel a few miles a day.	¶ We traveled in the snow from the last crossing of the Plat river. We had orders not to pass the handcart co. We had to keep close to them until help came or if we could help them. We began to get short of food and our cattle gave out. We could only travel a few miles a day.
39	When we started out of Camp in the morning, the Brethren would shovel the snow to make a track for our cattle where [were] weak for the want of food as the Buffalos where [were] in Large herds by the Roads and eat all the Grass.	When we started out of camp in the morning the brethren would shovel the snow to make a track for our cattle. They were weak for the want of food as the buffaloes were in large herds by the roads and ate all the grass.	When we started out of camp in the morning the brethren would shovel the snow to make a track for our cattle. They were weak for the want of food as the buffaloes were in large herds by the roads and ate all the grass.	When we started out of camp in the morning the brethren would shovel the snow to make a track for our cattle. They wee weak for the want of food as the buffaloes were in large herds. They were by the roads and ate all the grass.

#	Holograph	Larsen	Pay	Bowers
40	When we arrived at Devils Gate it was bitter Cold. We Left Lots of our things there. There was 2 or 3 Log houses there and we Left our wagon there and joined teams with a man the name of James Farmer. He had a sister Mary frozen to death.	¶ When we arrived at Devils Gate it was bitter cold. We left lots of our things there. There were two or three log houses there. We left our wagons and joined teams with man named James Barmen. He had a sister Mary frozen to death.	¶ When we arrived at Devils Gate it was bitter cold. We left lots of our things there. There were two or three log houses there. We left our wagons and joined teams with man named James Barman. He had a sister Mary frozen to death.	¶ When we arrived at Deviled Gate it was bitter cold. We left lots of our things there. There were two or three log houses there. We left our wagons and joined teams with man named James Barman. He had a sister Mary who froze to death.
41	We stayed there 2 or 3 days. While there an ox fell on the ice and the Brethren killed it and the Beef was given out to the camp. We make soup of it. My Br james eat a hearty supper was as well as he ever was wen he went to bed. In the morning he was dead.	We stayed there two or three days. While there an ox fell on the ice and the brethren killed it and the beef was given out to the camp. My brother James ate a hearty supper was well as he ever was when he went to bed. In the morning he was dead.	We stayed there two or three days. While there an ox fell on the ice and the brethren killed it and the beef was given out to the camp. My brother James ate a hearty supper and was well as he ever was when he went to bed. In the morning he was dead.	We stayed there two or three days. While there an ox fell on the ice and the brethren killed it and gave the beef out to the camp. My brother James ate a harty supper and was well as he ever was when he went to bed. The next morning he was dead.
42	I got my feet frozen and lost all my toes. My Br Edwin got his feet froze bad. [My] Sister Carrie feet where [were] froze. It was nothing but snow.	¶ My feet were frozen also my brother Edwin and my sister Carrie [Caroline penciled in] had their feet frozen. It was nothing but snow.	¶ My feet were frozen also my brother Edwin and my sister Caroline had their feet frozen. It was nothing but snow.	¶ My feet was frozen also my brother Edwin and my sister Caroline had their feet frozen. There was nothing but snow.

#	Holograph	Larsen	Pay	Bowers
43	We could not drive the p[e]gs in our tents. Father would clean a place for our tent put snow around to keep it down. We were short of flour But father was a good shot. They Called him the hunter of the camp so that helped us out.	¶ We could not drive the pegs in our tents. Father would clean a place for our tents and put snow around to keep it down. We were short of flour but father was a good shot. They called him the hunter of the camp, so that helped us out.	¶ We could not drive the pegs in our tents. Father would clean a place for our tents and put snow around to keep it down. We were short of flour but father was a good shot. They called him the hunter of the camp, so that helped us out.	¶ We could not drive the pegs in the ground for our tents. Father would clean a place for our tents and put snow around it to keep it down. We were short of flour but father was a good shot. They called him the hunter of the camp. So that help us out.
44	We could not get a enough flour for Bread as we got to a quarter lb per head a day. So we would make it Like thin Gruel. We called it skilly.	We could not get enough flour for bread as we got only a quarter of a pound per head a day so we would make it like thin gruel. We call it skilly.	We could not get enough flour for bread as we got only a quarter of a pound per head a day so we would make it like thin gruel. We call it skilly.	We could not get enough flour for bread as we got only a quarter of a pound per head a day so we would make it like thin gruel. We call it "skilly."

#	Holograph	Larsen	Pay	Bowers
45	Well there was 4 companies on the plains. We did not know what would become of us when one night a man came to our Camp telling us there would be plenty of flour in the morning for Br Brigham had sent men and teams to help us. There was rejoiceing that night: Some sang, some danced, some cried. Well he was a Living Santy Claus. I have forgotten his name but never will i forget how he looked. He was covered with the frost, his beard was Long and all frost. [*penciled below last line*] His name was Eph Hanks.	¶ There were four companies on the plains. We did not know what would become of us. One night a man came to our camp and told us there would be plenty of flour in the morning for Bro. Brigham Young had sent men and teams to help us. There was rejoicing that night. We sang songs, some danced and some cried. He was a living Santa Claus. His name was Eph. Hanks.	¶ There were four companies on the plains. We did not know what would become of us. One night a man came to our camp and told us there would be plenty of flour in the morning for Bro. Brigham Young had sent men and teams to help us. There was rejoicing that night. We sang songs, some danced and some cried. He was a living Santa Claus. His name was Eph. Hanks.	¶ There were four companies on the plains. We did not know what would become of us. One night a man came to our camp and told us there would be plenty of flour in the morning for Bro. Young had sent men and teams to help us. There was rejoicing that night. We sang songs and some danced and some cried. He was a living Santa Claus. His name was Eph. Hanks.
46	We travel faster now we had horse teams.	¶ We traveled faster now we had horse teams.	¶ We traveled faster now we had horse teams.	¶ We traveled faster now we had horse teams.

#	Holograph	Larsen	Pay	Bowers
47	See #33 and #34	¶ My mother had never got well, she lingered until the 11 of Dec., the day we arrived in Salt Lake City 1856. She died between the little and big mountains. She was buried in the Salt Lake City Cemetery. She was 43 years old. She and her baby lost their lives gathering to zion in such a late season of the year. My sister was buried at the last crossing of the Sweetwater.	¶ My mother had never got well, she lingered until the 11 of Dec., the day we arrived in Salt Lake City 1856. She died between the little and big mountains. She was buried in the Salt Lake City Cemetery. She was 43 years old. She and her baby lost their lives gathering to zion in such a late season of the year. My sister was buried at the last crossing of the Sweetwater.	My mother had never got well, she lingered until the 11 of December the day we arrived in Salt Lake City, 1856. She died between the little and big mountain. She was buried in the Salt Lake City, Cemetery. She was 43 years old. She and her baby lost their lives gathering to Zion in such a late season of the year. My sister was buried at the last crossing of the Sweetwater.
48	and we arrived in salt Lake City 9 o clock at night, the 11 of Dec 1856. 3 out of the 4 that was Living froze; my mother dead in the wagon.	¶ We arrived in Salt Lake City nine o'clock at night the 11th of Dec. 1856. Three out of the four that were living were frozen. My mother was dead in the wagon.	¶ We arrived in Salt Lake City nine o'clock at night the 11th of December 1856. Three out of the four that were living were frozen. My mother was dead in the wagon.	We arrived in Salt Lake City, nine o'clock at night the 11th of Dec. 1856. Three out of the four that were living were frozen. My mother was dead in the wagon.

#	Holograph	Larsen	Pay	Bowers
49	Bishop Handy had us taken to a house in his ward and the Brethren an sister fetch us plenty of food. We had to be careful and not eat to[o] much as it might Kill us as we were so hungry.	¶ Bishop Hardy had us taken to a house in his ward and the brethren and sisters brought us plenty of food. We had to be careful and not eat too much as it might kill us we were so hungry.	¶ Bishop Hardy had us taken to a house in his ward and the brethren and sisters brought us plenty of food. We had to be careful and not eat too much as it might kill us we were so hungry.	¶ Bishop Hardy had us taken to a home in his ward and the brethren and the sister brought us plenty of food. We had to be careful and not eat too much as it might kill us we were so hungry.
50	The next day the Bishop came and brought a docter. His name was Williams.	¶ Early next morning Bro. Brigham Young and a doctor came. The doctor's name was Williams. When Brigham Young came in he shook hands with all of us. When he saw our condition, our feet frozen and our mother dead, tears rolled down his cheeks.	¶ Early next morning Bro. Brigham Young and a doctor came. The doctor's name was Williams. When Brigham Young came in he shook hands with all of us. When he saw our condition, our feet frozen and our mother dead, tears rolled down his cheeks.	¶ Early next morning Bro. Brigham and a doctor came. The doctor's name was Williams. When Bro. Young came in he shook hands with all of us. When he saw our condition of our frozen feet and our dead mother, tears rolled down his cheeks.

#	Holograph	Larsen	Pay	Bowers
51	He amputated our feet.	¶ The Doctor wanted to cut my feet off at the ankle. But Pres. Young said no just cut off the toes and I promise you, you will never have to take them off any farther. The pieces of bone that must come out will work out through the skin themselves. ¶ The Doctor amputated my ~~feet~~ toes using a saw and a butcher knife.	¶ The Doctor wanted to cut my feet off at the ankles. But Pres. Young said no just cut off the toes and I promise you, you will never have to take them off any farther. The pieces of bone that must come out will work out through the skin themselves. ¶ The Doctor amputated my toes using a saw and a butcher knife.	¶ The doctor amputated my toes using a saw and a butcher knife. Brigham Young promised me I would not have to have any more of my feet cut off.
52	The sister where [were] dressing mother for her grave.	The sisters were dressing mother for her grave.	The sisters were dressing mother for her grave.	The sisters were dressing mother for the last time.
53	My poor father walk in the where Mother was, then back to us. He could not shed a tear. When our feet was fine they packed us in to see our mother for the Last time. Oh how did we stand it. That afternoon she was burried.	My poor father walked in the room where mother was then back to us. He could not shed a tear. When my feet were fixed they packed us in to see our mother for the last time. Oh how did we stand it. That afternoon she was buried.	My poor father walked in the room where mother was then back to us. He could not shed a tear. When my feet were fixed they packed us in to see our mother for the last time. Oh how did we stand it. That afternoon she was buried.	Oh how did we stand it. That afternoon she was buried.

[SEVERAL PAGES OMITTED]

#	Holograph	Larsen	Pay	Bowers
54	It is now Oct ~~1896~~ 1906, 50 years since we left our home over the sea for utah. Qu[i]te a few of us that are left have been to salt Lake City to Celebrate our Jubilee. We met in the 14 ward Assembly hall. Well h[e]ld 3 meetings. Pres Joseph F Smith and the R[elief] S[ociety] furnish us a Banquet.	¶ It is now Oct. ~~1896~~ 1906 fifty years ago we left our homes over the sea for Utah. Quite a few of us that are left have been to Salt Lake City to celebrate our Jubilee. We met in the 14th Ward Assembly Hall. We held three meetings. Pres. Joseph F. Smith presided and the Relief Society furnished us a Banquet.	¶ It is now Oct. 1906, fifty years ago we left our homes over the sea for Utah. Quite a few of us that are left have been to Salt Lake City to celebrate our Jubilee. We met in the 14th ward Assembly Hall. We held three meetings. President Joseph F. Smith presided and the Relief Society furnished us a Banquet.	¶ It is now Oct. 1896 Forty years ago we left our homes over the sea for Utah. Quite a few of us that are left have been in Salt Lake City to celebrate our Jubilee. We met in the 14th ward assembly Hall. We held three meeting. President Joseph F. Smith presided and the Relief Society furnished us a banquet.
55	We had a good time. I staid with anna pay Kimball. We met the Capt of our company, Br Jhon [John] Hunt met some of the people that came in our Company. We were happy to see one another and talked of the times that are gone	We had a very good time. I stayed with Annie Pay Kimball. We met the Captain of our company Bro John Hunt and some of the people that came in our company. We were happy to see one another and talk of the times that are gone.	We had a very good time. I stayed with Annie Pay Kimball. We met the captain of our company, Brother John Hunt and some of the people that came in our company. We were happy to see one another and talk of the times that are gone.	We had a very good time. I stayed with Annie Pay Kimball. We met the captain of our company. We were happy to see one another and talk of the time that are gone.
56	My sister Carrie and husband went up to the city with us. Her husband came in Capt Elsworths Hand Cart Company.	¶ My sister Carrie and her husband went up to the city with me. Her husband ~~went~~ came in Captain Ellsworth's Hand Cart Company.	¶ My sister Carrie and her husband went up to the city with me. Her husband came in Captain Ellsworth's Hand Cart Company.	¶ My sister Carrie and her husband went up to the City with us. Her husband came in Captain Ellsworth Hand cart Co.

#	Holograph	Larsen	Pay	Bowers
57	went to Conference two Days than went to the Cemetry to find my mothers grave. It was Lot 2 plat C. It was the first time i had seen it, for when she was burried our feet were so bad we could not go to the funeral and the move came and we moved south to Nephi.	¶ We went to Conference two days then went to the cemetery to find my mother's grave. It was Lot 2 plot C. It was the first time I had seen it for when she was buried our feet were so we could not go to the funeral and later we moved South.	¶ We went to Conference two days then went to the cemetery to find my mother's grave. It was in Lot 2, plot C. It was the first time I had seen it, for when she was buried our feet were so we could not go to the funeral and later we moved south.	¶ We went to conference two days then went to the cemetery to find my mother's grave. It was in Lot 2, plot C. It was the first time I had seen it: for when she was burried our feet were so we could not go to the funeral and later we moved south.
58	No one noes [knows] how i felt as we stood there by her grave. There were Alma, his wife, myself an[d] Ethel one of George Daughters. There were 3 generations. Our mother was a martyr for the truth.	¶ No one knows how I felt as we stood there by her grave. There were Alma, his wife, myself, and Ethel, one of George's daughters. There were three generations and now our mother was a martyr for the truth.	¶ No one knows how I felt as we stood there by her grave. There was Alma, his wife, myself and Ethel, one of George's daughters. There were three generations and our mother was a martyr to for the truth.	¶ No one knows how I felt as we stood there by her grave. There was Alma, His wife, Myself, and Ethel, one of George daughters. There was three generations and our mother was a martyr for the truth.

#	Holograph	Larsen	Pay	Bowers
59	I thought of her words, Polly i want to go to Zion while my Children are small so as they can be raised in the gospel of Christ for i know this is the true Church. Now there are 31 grand children 26 g Grand Children Living an 15 are dead. There are 3 of us Living: my Bro, sister and myself.	¶ I thought of her words, Polly, I want to go to Zion while my children are small so they can be raised in the Gospel of Christ for I know this is the true church. ¶ Now there are 31 grand children 36 great grand children living and 15 are dead. There are three of us living my brother, sister and I.	¶ I though[t] of her words, "Polly, I want to go to Zion while my children are small, so they can be raised in the Gospel of Christ for I know this is the true church." ¶ Now there are 31 grandchildren, 36 great grandchildren living and 15 are dead. There are three of us living my brother, sister and I.	I thought of her words, Polly, I want to go to Zion while my children are small, so they can be raised in the Gospel of Christ. For I know this is the true Church. ¶ Now there are 31 grandchildrens, 36 great grandchildren living and 15 are dead. There are three of us living my brother sister, and I.
	[PARAGRAPH OMITTED]			
60	I think my mother has her wish. My Br and 3 of my sons have filled missions and some of her grandsons and daughters are workers in the Church. They all are members of the Church.	¶ I think my mother had her wish. My brother and three of my sons have filled missions and her grandsons and daughters are workers in the church. They all are members of the church.	¶ I think my mother had her wish. My brother and three of my sons have filled missions and her grandsons and daughters are workers in the church. They are all members of the church.	I think my mother had her wish. My brother and three of my sons have filled missions and her grandsons and daughters are worker in the church.
61	I now have 6 sons and 1 daughter Living, 4 sons are married, and i have 11 grand-children and i am proud of them all.	¶ I now have six sons and one daughter living, four sons are married and I have eleven grand children and I am proud of them all.	¶ I now have six sons and one daughter living, four sons are married and I have eleven grandchildren and I am proud of them all.	¶ I now have six sons and one daughter living, four sons are married and I have eleven grand children and I am proud of them all.

#	Holograph	Larsen	Pay	Bowers
62	I am the mother of 13 children, 10 sons 3 Daughters. My Br Edwin is the father of 15 sons and Daughters. My sis Carrie Bowers the mother of 9, 5 sons 4 daughters. My sis Harriet the mother of 9. 7 sons 2 daughters.	¶ I am the mother of thirteen children 10 sons and three daughters. My Bro. Edwin is the father of fifteen sons and daughters. My sister Carrie is the mother of nine children five sons and four daughters and my sister Harriet the mother of nine, seven sons and two daughters.	¶ I am the mother of thirteen children, 10 sons and three daughters. My Bro. Edwin is the father of fifteen sons and daughters. My sister Carrie is the mother of nine children, five sons and four daughters and my sister Harriet the mother of nine, seven sons and two daughters.	¶ I am the mother of thirteen children, 10 sons and three daughters. My Bro. Edwin is the fathers of fifteen sons and daughters. My sister Carrie is the mother of nine— seven sons and two daughters.
	[PARAGRAPH OMITTED]			
63	Nephi, Oct 1908 have been to our hand cart renion I met quite a few old friends went to Conference. My Bro and i went to see mothers grave. They had Remembered them. It is plot f Lot 8 or12. We will have it fixed, leveled and grass sown of it.	¶ Oct. 1908, I have been to our Hand Cart reunion and met quite a few old friends. We went to Conference in Salt Lake and my brother and I went to see mother's grave. It has been renumbered. It is now plot F, Lot 8 and 12.	¶ Oct. 1908, I have been to our Hand Cart reunion and met quite a few old friends. We went to Conference in Salt Lake and my brother and I went to see mother's grave. It has been renumbered. It is now Plot F, Lot 8 and 12.	¶ Oct. 1908, I have been to our handcart Reunion and met quite a few old friends. We went to conference in Salt Lake City. Then my brother and I went to see mother grave. It has been renumber. It is now Plot F. Lot 8 and 12.

#	Holograph	Larsen	Pay	Bowers
64	Oct 21 1909 Went to Sunday School was asked to relate incidents of our journey across the plains. I told we had the first snow storm the 22 September 1856. There were 15 died through Crossing that platte river. Sis Mcphersen sat by me. She said my mother was the 15 one that died. They were laid side by side and a Little dirt threw over them.	¶ Oct. 24, 1909 I went to Sunday School and was asked to relate a few incidents of our journey across the plains. I told them we had the first snow storm the 22nd of Sept. in 1856. There were fifteen who died through the cold and exposure while crossing the Platte River. Sister McPherson sat by me and she said her mother was the fifteenth to die. They were all laid side by side and a little dirt thrown over them.	¶ Oct. 24, 1909 I went to Sunday School and was asked to relate a few incidents of our journey across the plains. I told them we had the first snow storm the 22nd of Sept. in 1856. There were fifteen who died through the cold and exposure while crossing the Platte River. Sister McPherson sat by me and she said her mother was the fifteenth to die. They were all laid side by side and a little dirt thrown over them.	¶ Oct. 24, 1909, I went to Sunday School and was asked to relate a few incidents of our journey acroos the plains. I told them we had the first snow storm of the year on the 22 Sept 1856. There were fifteen who died through the cold and exposure while crossing the platte river. Sister McPerson sat by me and she said her mother was the fifteenth one. They were all laid side by side and a little dirt thrown over them.
65	Nov. have been to our renion. Met at Br Langly Baily. Had a good time. Told of incidents of our trip over the plains. It made us feel bad. It brought it all up again. Is it wise, yes, for our Children to see what there parents passed through for the Gospel.	November, I have been to reunion. I met Bro. Langly Bailey and had a good time talking over incidents of our trip across the plains. It made me feel bad it brought it all up again. Is it wise for our children to see what their parents passed through for the Gospel. Yes I think it is.	¶ November, I have been to reunion. I met Bro. Langly Bailey and had a good time talking over incidents of our trip across the plains. It made me feel bad. It brought it all up again. Is it wise for our children to see what their parents passed through for the gospel? Yes, I think it is.	¶ November, I have been to reunion, I met Bro Langly Bailey and had a good time talking over incidents of our trip across the plains. It made me feel bad it brought it all up again. Is it wise for our children to see what their parents passed through for the gospel, Yes I think it is.

Appendix 2

Letter from Mary Goble Pay to Samuel Stephen Jones, 18 October 1908

Transcription of a letter from Mary Goble Pay to Samuel Stephen Jones. Jones had been chairperson of the Handcart Veterans "Jubilee" celebration held in Salt Lake City on the 4th through the 6th of October 1906 and had requested information in preparation for another reunion of handcart veterans. The original letter is housed in the Church History Library (MS 11378, Handcart Veterans Association scrapbook, 1906–1914). Letter transcribed by Jay G. Burrup, 24 March 2006 (with punctuation added by the author).

Mr. S. S. Jones
Provo, Utah
Oct 18, 1908

Dear Bro.,

I will now try and send you a little of our history as you requested. My parents' names were William and Mary Goble. There were 6 children: Mary, Edwin, Caroline, Harriet, James and Fanny. We left our home in Brighton, Sussex, England May 19, 1856. Came to London that day, the next to Liverpool. Went on board the ship *Horizon* that night. Sailed on the 25th. When we were in the river the crew mutinied. They fought terrible. They were put ashore and another crew came on board. When we were in the banks of Newfoundland we were in a fog. All at once the clouds parted. We were close to a large iceberg. It look[ed] like a mountain. The sun shone till the ship was out of danger, [t]hen the fog closed in again.

We landed in Boston [and] took a train for Iowa Camp Ground. My sister died the 19 of July 1856 on Iowa Camp Ground. She was 2 years all but 4 days. [She] took cold through getting wet. She was just getting over the measles. We left about the 20 to travel through the states in Capt. J. Hunt's wagon company to Council Bluffs. We started for the plains Sep. 1, 1856.

The 23 of Sep. my mother was confined with a little girl. We named her Edith and she died and was buried [at] the Last crossing of the Sweetwater for want of nourishment. Our mother never got well. She linger[e]d for 11 weeks and died the 11 December 1856 between the Big and Little Mountain about 4 o'clock in the afternoon. She was buried in the City Cemetery. I rode in the same bed with my dead mother til 9 o'clock that night.

My brother James was frozen in his bed at Devil's Gate. [He] went to bed well [and] in the morning was dead. There were father and 4 of us left—3 out of the 4 froze[n]. I lost all my toes, brother Edwin lost part of his toes, and Carrie part of her big toes. We were told to stay and help the handcart companies. My father shared his provision with the company. That made us short and we suffered with the rest.

I saw an inquiry about Bro. Stone. My husband R[ichard] Pay was driving the cattle up one morning. Some of them ran in the brush. He went after them. He saw a part of a man's leg and arm and his vest. His watch was in his pocket. He came to camp and notified Capt. Hunt and Spencer, and they went with him to the place. It looked like he was tired and sat down to rest. Br. Pay gave the watch to his sister. I have forgotten her name. They came to Spanish Fork. Her daughter's name was Anna. She married Bishop Wells of Spanish Fork. I knew Bro. Stone well. He would often stay to our camp with his sister.

Now Bro. Jones, I hope you can make this out. This is [as] correct as I can tell it from memory. Hoping you will take the part out that you want.

From Mrs. Mary G. Pay
Nephi City, Juab Co., Utah

[Postscript written across top margin of page 5:]

My husband, Richard Pay, buried his baby girl at Chimney Rock and his [first] wife, Sarah, at Bridger. His feet were froze[n] very bad. He arrived in Salt Lake 14 December 1856.

Appendix 3

Comparative Chronology of Willie and Martin Handcart Companies, Hunt Wagon Company, and Rescue Companies

The Hodgetts wagon company did not keep a separate camp journal; therefore, the company is not included in this comparative chronology, though it generally traveled within a day of the Martin company.

The "Rescuers" column focuses primarily on the initial company led by George D. Grant (based primarily on "Robert T. Burton diaries, 1856–1907," Record book, circa 1856 October–November; CHL, MS 1221), but it includes some information on rescuers who followed Grant. Numerous groups and individuals left the Salt Lake Valley to assist in the rescue during October and November, with the last supply train leaving on 2 December 1856. This column also includes the movement of others, such as Franklin D. Richards.

Date	Willie	Martin	Hunt	Rescuers
4 May	*Thornton* sails from Liverpool.			
19 May			William Goble family leaves Brighton.	
25 May		*Horizon* sails from Liverpool.	*Horizon* sails from Liverpool.	
14 June	*Thornton* arrives in New York.			
26 June	Arrive in Iowa city.			
30 June		*Horizon* arrives in Boston.	*Horizon* arrives in Boston.	
1 July		Passengers disembark in Boston.	Passengers disembark in Boston.	
9 July		Arrive in Iowa City.	Arrive in Iowa City.	
13 July			Fifth wagon company organized with Dan Jones, captain.	
15 July	Depart Iowa City.			
19 July			Fanny Goble (twenty-three months) dies in Iowa Camp.	
22 July		Company leaves Iowa City.		
1 Aug.			Company begins leaving Iowa City campground about 4:00 p.m. and travels two miles.	

Date	Willie	Martin	Hunt	Rescuers
4 Aug.			Company stabilizes at fifty-six wagons.	
11 Aug.	Arrive in Florence.			
10 Aug.			John A. Hunt appointed captain.	
13 Aug.	Decide not to stay the winter in Florence.			
14 Aug.			Dan Jones leaves the company.	
16 Aug.	Leave Florence.			
22 Aug.		Company arrives in Florence. Haven and Martin companies combined into a single company.		
25 Aug.		Leave Florence with about 620 members.		
28 Aug.			Ferry Missouri River and arrive in Florence.	
31 Aug.			Leave Florence.	
3 Sept.				Franklin D. Richards and party leave Florence.
5 Sept.			Receive report of Indian attack on Babbitt company.	
6 Sept.			Franklin D. Richards passes the Hunt company at about 10:15AM.	

Date	Willie	Martin	Hunt	Rescuers
7 Sept.		Franklin D. Richards passes the Martin Company.	Franklin D. Richards passes the Hodgetts company about ten miles past the Martin company.	
12 Sept.	Franklin D. Richards meets the company.			
13 Sept.		Arrive at Fort Kearny, Nebraska.		
15 Sept.			"The weather being very hot, the cattle suffered much."	Franklin D. Richards meets the Smoot Company and notes they had provisions for twenty-three days.
				Richards meets O. P. Rockwell with five wagons. At Fort Laramie, Richards "purchased some good buffalo robes for the P.E. Fund passengers in the rear."
18 Sept.	"Very sharp frost." Camp on Platte at Ash Hollow.			
23 Sept.			"Cold and frosty." A buffalo is shot in the afternoon, and the meat is distributed.	Richards "purchased a few more robes for Capt. J. G. Willie's company" at Platte Bridge.

Date	Willie	Martin	Hunt	Rescuers
24 Sept.	Pass Chimney Rock.		Mary Penfold Goble gives birth to baby, Edith, before leaving camp in the morning.	Richards meets John Smith who was bringing flour out, presumably for the Smoot company.
27 Sept.				Richards meets William Smith fifteen miles east of Pacific Springs with two wagons of flour. He counsels him to cache his flour and go on to meet the Willie company.
30 Sept.	At Fort Laramie.			
4 Oct. (Sat.)	Rations are reduced. Passed by Parley P. Pratt and other missionaries going east.	Pass Scott's Bluff.	Sussanah Bruner (64) dies. Pass Chimney Rock about 10:00 a.m. Marinda Nancy Pay (ten weeks old) dies just before midnight.	Franklin D. Richards meets with First Presidency in Salt Lake City; decision made to organize relief party immediately.
5 Oct. (Sun.)			Passed by Parley P. Pratt and other missionaries going east.	Brigham Young calls for relief party volunteers to leave as soon as possible.
6 Oct. (Mon.)			John Turley (forty-two) dies. Ruth Jones born. Pass Scott's Bluff.	

Appendix 3

105

Date	Willie	Martin	Hunt	Rescuers
7 Oct. (Tues.)			Cattle stampede, damaging William Goble's wagon. Esther Walters is trampled, dies, leaving four-week-old infant.	First members of rescue party leave Salt Lake City, camp near Big Mountain.
8 Oct. (Wed.)		Reach Fort Laramie		
9 Oct. (Thurs.)			John Joseph Wiseman, age five, dies from "bodily weakness."	
10 Oct. (Fri.)	Reach Platte Crossing, obtain thirty-six buffalo robes at trading post, which had been arranged by Franklin D. Richards.		At Fort Laramie.	
11 Oct. (Sat.)			Trading at Fort Laramie, then resume journey.	
12 Oct. (Sun.)			Travel seven miles. Brothers Bell and Beesley return to Fort Laramie due to lateness of the season.	Arrive at Fort Bridger.
13 Oct. (Mon.)	Pass Willow Springs and Prospect Hill, camp at Greasewood Creek.	Travel twenty miles, camp two miles from North Platte River.	Travel twenty miles.	Leave Fort Bridger, camp on Black's Fork.

Date	Willie	Martin	Hunt	Rescuers
14 Oct. (Tues.)	Travel thirteen miles, camp one mile west of Independence Rock.	Travel twenty miles, just behind the Hodgetts company.	Travel fifteen miles.	Send express from Black's Fork: Joseph A. Young, Cyrus H. Wheelock, Steven Taylor, Abel Garr.
15 Oct. (Wed.)	Caroline Reeder (seventeen) dies. Travel sixteen miles, passing Devil's Gate; rations are further reduced to 10.5 oz. for men, 9 oz. for women and large children, 6 oz. for small children, 3 oz. for infants.		Ford Platte, travel seventeen miles.	Travel past Green River to Big Sandy.
16 Oct. (Thurs.)	Three deaths and one birth. Travel eleven miles, camp just west of Split Rock.		Travel twenty-two miles, ford to south side of Platte.	Camp at Big Sandy. Meet up with Smoot wagon train.
17 Oct. (Fri.)	One death. Travel thirteen miles, ford Sweetwater.	Baggage is reduced to 10 pounds per adult, 5 pounds per child. Blankets, clothing, etc. are burned to lighten load. Camp at Deer Creek.	Travel sixteen miles.	Camp at Little Sandy.
18 Oct. (Sat.)	One death. Travel eight miles, ford Sweetwater (fourth crossing).		Travel fifteen miles.	Cross South Pass and camp at head of the Sweetwater.

Appendix 3

Date	Willie	Martin	Hunt	Rescuers
19 Oct. (Sun.)	One death before leaving, four during the day. Pass ice slough, snowstorm hits early in the day, meet express just west of ice slough, eat last of flour, camp at sixth crossing of Sweetwater.	Arrive at last crossing of Platte. Hodgetts company crosses, followed by Martin company, assisted by Hunt company. Storm hits in the evening.	Travel fourteen miles, passing "Fort Bridge" (near the Platte Bridge) and camp at last crossing of the Platte. Hunt company meets up with Martin company there and assists them in crossing Platte.	Very cold. Hit by storm in evening. Express riders meet the Willie company, then continue on in search of Martin, Hunt, and Hodgetts companies. Redick Allred establishes a base camp at head of the Sweetwater.
20 Oct. (Mon.)	One death; four to five inches of snow on ground. Company stays in camp on Sweetwater, east of Rocky Ridge at sixth crossing of Sweetwater. Willie and Elder leave about 10:00 a.m. to search for the rescue party.	Trapped by snow, stay in camp. Fourteen die at this camp.	Trapped by snow, stay in camp. "It commenced snowing again at 3:00 p.m. and continued for some time."	Willie and Elder directed to camp of rescue party by signboard left on road. Willie and Elder meet rescuers at night, about twenty-five miles west of the Willie company camp.
21 Oct. (Tues.)	Stay in camp. Four deaths. Willie arrives with fourteen relief wagons about sunset. Nine buried at this camp.	Move about five miles to Emigrant Gap Ridge.	Trapped by snow, stay in camp. Snow eight inches deep.	Leave early in morning with relief wagons and meet Willie company about sunset. "Snow deep."

Date	Willie	Martin	Hunt	Rescuers
22 Oct. (Wed.)	Travel eleven miles with six relief wagons. Camp on Sweetwater. Two deaths.	Trapped by snow, stay in camp at Emigrant Gap Ridge.	Ford Platte about 1:00 p.m. and camp about one mile beyond the ford. Several cattle die.	Travel seventeen miles through deep snow with eight to ten wagons. Camp at Wallahualtah Rock, at base of Rocky Ridge.
23 Oct. (Thurs.)	Travel sixteen miles up Rocky Ridge, cold and windy, some do not arrive in camp until daybreak. Two deaths.	Move a few miles to Red Buttes, where the Hodgetts company is camped.	Trapped by snow, stay in camp. "Very cold and frosty."	"Snow deep. Could not travel."
24 Oct. (Fri.)	Thirteen burials in the morning. Stay in camp. Six relief wagons arrive.	Trapped by snow, stay in camp at Red Buttes.	Trapped by snow, stay in camp. "A very cold northwest wind blowing."	Travel beyond Three Crossings through deep snow.
25 Oct. (Sat.)	Two deaths; travel fifteen miles, crossing Sweetwater for last time.	Trapped by snow, stay in camp at Red Buttes. Flour rations are reduced to 8 oz. per adult and 4 oz. per child.	Trapped by snow, stay in camp.	
26 Oct. (Sun.)	Two deaths; travel fourteen miles, crossing South Pass. Camp on Pacific Creek.	Trapped by snow, stay in camp at Red Buttes.	Trapped by snow, stay in camp. Capt. Hunt goes to Fort Bridge to see about purchasing more cattle.	Arrive at Devil's Gate, where express party is waiting. In Salt Lake City, Church leaders call for more men and wagons to assist.

Date	Willie	Martin	Hunt	Rescuers
27 Oct. (Mon.)	Travel eighteen miles, camp on Little Sandy.	Trapped by snow, stay in camp at Red Butte. Elizabeth Horrocks Jackson (whose husband died the night of 25 Oct) sees husband in a dream who says, "Cheer up, Elizabeth. Deliverance is at hand."	Trapped by snow, stay in camp. Capt. Hunt returns with sixteen cattle.	Stay at Devil's Gate while express (Joseph A. Young, Dan Jones, Abel Garr) goes east looking for Martin and Hunt companies. Probable date of Ephraim Hanks' departure.
28 Oct. (Tues.)	Travel eight miles, camp on Big Sandy.	A "red letter day": express arrives with news that supplies are at Devil's Gate.	Express arrives in camp. "Continued cold." Thirteen more cattle brought from the fort.	Express connects with Hodgetts, Martin, Hunt companies, in that order. Relief wagons remain at Devil's Gate.
29 Oct. (Wed.)	Two deaths; travel fifteen miles, camp on Big Sandy.	Travel to Avenue of Rocks.	Travel three miles.	Express camps with Martin company.
30 Oct. (Thurs.)	Two deaths; travel eleven miles, cross Green River.	Camp at Willow Springs.	Travel seven miles to Red Buttes. Margaret Price gives birth to a daughter.	Express returns to Devil's Gate and reports location of Martin, Hodgetts, and Hunt companies.
31 Oct. (Fri.)	Travel eighteen miles. Ten more supply wagons arrive.	Rescuers Wheelock, Jones, and Garr return in afternoon. Camp at Greasewood Creek, where six relief wagons arrive.	Remain in camp all day.	Move relief wagons to Greasewood Creek, where they meet Martin company.

Date	Willie	Martin	Hunt	Rescuers
1 Nov. (Sat.)	One death; travel fifteen miles, meet more relief wagons.	Camp near Independence Rock. Deep snow has to be cleared away to set up camp.	Travel twelve miles (through Bad Water area). Meet C. H. Wheelock and William Broomhead from rescue party, camp at Avenue of Rocks. "Snow and rain."	Begin moving back toward Devil's Gate. "Snowed until late at night; camped near Independence Rock."
2 Nov. (Sun.)	One death in evening; travel fifteen miles, passing Fort Bridger. Ephraim Hanks passes the company.	Arrive at Devil's Gate late in the evening.	Travel four miles to Willow Springs, snow six to seven inches deep. "Very cold." Probably where Mary is lost in snow.	Camp at Devil's Gate. "Snow very deep, very cold."
3 Nov. (Mon.)	Travel about twelve miles, passing more relief wagons. Camp on Muddy Creek. All are now able to ride in wagons.	Remain at Devil's Gate. One death reported.	"Very cold." Travel eleven miles, camp at Greasewood Creek. "The infant child of William Goble died at 9 o'clock p.m."	Too cold to travel, remain at Devil's Gate. Send express (J. A. Young and Abel Garr) to Salt Lake City requesting additional help.
4 Nov. (Tues.)	W. H. Kimball and Thomas sent to Salt Lake City. Ford Bear River and camp on Bear. Pass several relief wagons.	Unload baggage at Devil's Gate, then move to Martin's Ravine (Cove), crossing the Sweetwater.	Travel five miles along Greasewood Creek.	Assist in building fires, setting up tents, cooking, etc., as well as unloading and storing baggage at Devil's Gate. Assist Martin company in crossing Sweetwater.

Date	Willie	Martin	Hunt	Rescuers
5 Nov. (Wed.)	Two deaths; travel twenty-three miles into Echo Canyon.	Camp at Martin's Cove. Three deaths reported.	Leave about 11:00 a.m., pass Independence Rock about 2:00 p.m., and arrive at Devil's Gate at 8:00 p.m., having traveled twelve miles. Meeting held to discuss leaving baggage and consolidating wagons. Jan Walters (eight weeks) dies.	At Devil's Gate and surrounding area.
6 Nov. (Thurs.)	Two deaths; ford Weber River; snowed all day.	Camp at Martin's Cove.	"Intense cold and stormy." Spend day unpacking wagons. William Burton (twenty-six) dies—"could not bear the intensity of the cold."	Record temperature of 11 degrees below zero at Devil's Gate. "So cold the people could not travel."
7 Nov. (Fri.)	Three deaths; camp in East Canyon, pass several relief wagons headed east.	Camp at Martin's Cove.	"Extremely cold." Continue unloading wagons. Ann Davis (forty-seven) dies. James Goble (four) dies at Devil's Gate, but the exact date is unrecorded.	At Devil's Gate. "Remained very cold. Could not travel. Stowing away goods, trying to save the people, stock, etc."
8 Nov. (Sat.)	One death; camp between Big and Little Mountains.	Camp at Martin's Cove.	Hodgetts company rolls out from Devil's Gate; Hunt continues to unload.	Begin to move out from Devil's Gate.

Date	Willie	Martin	Hunt	Rescuers
9 Nov. (Sun.)	One death; arrive in Salt Lake City.	Two deaths; leave Martin's Cove and resume journey. In addition to the four deaths reported in the Pioneer Database during the days at Martin's Cove, another nine deaths are listed for November with no specific date.	Leave Devil's Gate at noon, cross Sweetwater, travel six miles, and camp at 4:00 p.m. There are now twenty-four wagons in the company.	Daniel W. Jones, Thomas Alexander, Ben Hampton, and seventeen members of the Hodgetts and Hunt companies selected to remain behind and guard luggage over the winter. Seven teams that had left Salt Lake City after 26 Oct. turn back.
10 Nov. (Mon.)		Ephraim Hanks comes into camp with fresh buffalo meat.	Continue to move out from Devil's Gate.	Last wagon leaves Devil's Gate about 3:00 p.m. Ephraim Hanks meets the Martin company about dusk.
11 Nov. (Tues.)		Camp at Bitter Cottonwood Creek.	Mary Hutchinson (seventy) and James Reese (sixty) die.	Main group catches up to the Martin company. Brigham Young, hearing that some supply wagons had turned back, sends four men to intercept them with orders to turn around.
12 Nov. (Wed.)		Camp west of three crossings.	Sophie Turner (fourteen) dies.	Send an express to South Pass to obtain more supply wagons.

Date	Willie	Martin	Hunt	Rescuers
13 Nov. (Thurs.)		Four teams carrying flour arrive from South Pass. Travel sixteen miles, camp on Sweetwater near ice slough.		Express returns with four teams and some flour. Brigham Young receives letter from Grant requesting additional assistance.
14 Nov. (Fri.)		Camp on Sweetwater a few miles east of sixth crossing. First day without deaths since crossing the Platte near Casper.		
15 Nov. (Sat.)		Travel eight miles, camp on Sweetwater.		
16 Nov. (Sun.)		Cross Rocky Ridge; meet ten relief teams; bitter storm all day. Rations increased to 16 oz. per adult and 8 oz. per child.	John Turner (twelve) dies.	Ten more teams arrive from the valley.
17 Nov. (Mon.)		Sixteen deaths, all buried at Aspen Grove—worst single night for deaths.		

Date	Willie	Martin	Hunt	Rescuers
18 Nov. (Tues.)		Travel five miles, camp on Sweetwater near present site of Rock Hollow monument; meet Redick Allred. There are now enough wagons that all can ride.		Redick Allred meets the Martin company with additional wagons.
19 Nov. (Wed.)		Camp at Little Sandy.	Cross South Pass and camp at Pacific Springs.	
20 Nov. (Thurs.)		Camp on Big Sandy. Enough relief wagons that all can ride, but some walk to stay warm.	Company divides in several small groups.	
21 Nov. (Fri.)		At Black's Fork, more relief wagons arrive. Wagons spread out some distance, traveling at their own speed.	"Four horse teams arrived in camp this morning and took away about ten of our company to each wagon."	Additional wagons arrive with flour.
22 Nov. (Sat.)			"A number of oxen came from Fort Bridger and took several of our wagons to that place."	Additional teams arrive. Send some teams back to Hunt company.
23 Nov. (Sun.)		Arrive at Fort Bridger; snows in the evening.		Church leaders in Salt Lake City ask for more teams and wagons to assist.
24 Nov. (Mon.)		Muddy Creek, very cold.		
25 Nov. (Tues.)		Bear River.		

Date	Willie	Martin	Hunt	Rescuers
26 Nov. (Wed.)		Head of Echo Canyon.	Arrive at Green River.	
27 Nov. (Thurs.)		Weber River.	Sarah Pay (age thirty) dies.	
28 Nov. (Fri.)		East Canyon.		
29 Nov. (Sat.)		Camp at head of Emigration Canyon.	Several wagons cross the Green River.	Pass over Big Mountain in heavy snowstorm; pass over Little Mountain, camp at head of Emigration Canyon.
30 Nov. (Sun.)		Arrive in Salt Lake City about noon in 104 wagons.	Remaining wagons cross the Green River.	After arriving with the Martin company, Feramorz Little and Ephraim Hanks start east with the mail.
1 Dec. (Mon.)				
2 Dec. (Tues.)			Some wagons begin arriving at Fort Bridger.	Sixty more wagons leave Salt Lake City to assist in bringing in the Hodgetts and Hunt companies.
3 Dec. (Wed.)				
4 Dec. (Thurs.)			Last wagons arrive at Fort Bridger.	
5 Dec. (Fri.)				

Date	Willie	Martin	Hunt	Rescuers
6 Dec. (Sat.)			At Fort Bridger, messenger from Salt Lake City arrives with news that more teams are on the way. "This caused great joy in the camp."	
7 Dec. (Sun.)			At Fort Bridger, fourteen relief wagons arrive in the evening.	Fourteen relief wagons arrive at Fort Bridger.
8 Dec. (Mon.)			At Fort Bridger, more relief wagons arrive.	Additional relief wagons arrive at Fort Bridger.
9 Dec. (Tues.)			Some wagons resume journey to the valley.	Relief wagons begin carrying emigrants to the valley.
11 Dec. (Thurs.)			Mary Penfold Goble dies between Big and Little Mountains about 4:00 p.m. Surviving Gobles arrive in Salt Lake City at 9:00 p.m.	
13 Dec. (Sat.)			Richard Pay arrives in Salt Lake City.	
15 Dec. (Mon.)			"The remainder of the Saints arrived in Great Salt Lake City today, the emigration now being completed." Fifty wagons with 360 Saints arrived between 7 Dec and 15 Dec.	Rescue parties complete mission, except for those who remain behind at Devil's Gate to guard belongings left there.

Appendix 4

Hunt Company Camp Journal

From Journal History of The Church of Jesus Christ of Latter-day Saints, 15 December 1856, 16–37. It appears that this typed version of the camp journal was created in February 1926 and was included in the Journal History (see entry for 3 November 1926).

> < > = Insertions written in transcript
> deleted = Deletions written in transcript
> [ ] = Insertions added for clarification

The two wagon companies led by Captains William B. Hodgetts and John A. Hunt traveled close together while crossing the plains, and it appears that a camp journal was kept in the interests of both companies. It is not known who wrote the journal, but the following is a copy of it giving an account of the journeyings from Iowa City to the Salt Lake Valley:

Sunday, July 13. A meeting was held in the Latter-day Saint emigrant camp near Iowa City, at which a wagon company was organized for crossing the Plains to Great Salt Lake City, and the following officers were chosen: Dan Jones, captain of Hundred; John A. Hunt and William B. Hodgetts, captains of Fifties, Nathan Davis, Henry H. Dalrymple, Charles Roper, Nathan T. Porter, John Lewis, John Swenson, <Spencer> Gilbert, Thomas Thomas, captains of Tens; John Goodsall, chaplain; John Price, marshal, and Charles Holley, captain of the guard. At another meeting held the same day, Dan Jones presiding, further arrangements were made and instructions given for the future well-being of the company. It was considered necessary for a mule to be taken along for guarding and hunting cattle, etc., and it was proposed by Dan Jones that a subscription to be taken to purchase one for the company, which motion was carried unanimously. Brothers Smith and Billows and Tools were suggested to be on hand to assist in case of accidents happening to any of the wagons. Brother Thomas Parker said he would buy a smith, anvil, etc., on condition that the company would buy a mule to haul the same. It was further proposed by Dan Jones that such tools be purchased and a subscription taken for the purpose.

Wednesday, July 23. Some of the wagons moved off and camped about 2 miles out on the prairie, where they remained until the remainder of the company came up. Wednesday, July 30. Three companies of Tens under Charles Roper, Nathan T. Porter and John Swensen left the camp-ground in charge of William B. Hodgetts, to make their way to Council Bluffs separately, and not wait for the remainder of the company.

Thursday, July 31. Early this morning a messenger arrived with a petition of the company of thirty wagons which had left the camp-ground the day before <in [the] charge of Capt. Hodgett> for the use of the mule bought for the good of the company, as through the unruliness of their cattle, they could not get along without it. A meeting of captains of Tens was at once called, and it was unanimously resolved that considering the circumstances of the <Hodgetts Company> having the advantage of being in advance of the remaining part of the company, and cattle were now missing which caused the detention of the rear part of the company, they could not spare the mule, and send word accordingly.

Friday, August 1. The main company <(in [the] charge of Capt. Dan Jones)> left the camp ground near Iowa City at 4 o'clock p.m. and camped for the night, having traveled two miles. The encampment was made at a place where there was plenty of good feed for the cattle, but good drinking water was not to be had.

Saturday, August 2. The main company remained in camp all day, as some of the wagons belonging to the company were still behind.

Sunday, August 3. A general search was made for two yoke of oxen belonging to Mary Smith, and a muley [mule] ox belonging to William Busley. Men and oxen were sent back and every wagon was brought from the last camp ground [campground]. All the lost oxen were recovered. A meeting was called at 8 o'clock p.m. and addressed by Captain Dan Jones and others. Good and timely instructions were given to guide the emigrants in the prosecution of their journey.

Monday, August 4. The company resumed the journey at 10 o'clock a.m. with <their> fifty-six wagons which now comprised this part of the wagon company. A distance of six miles was covered and the night encampment made where there <was> water and excellent feed for the cattle.

Tuesday, August 5. The company started at 9 o'clock a.m., traveled over a good road 16 miles (resting an hour in the middle of the day), and camped for the night on high ground in the midst of small trees and near a creek, where there was good feed for the cattle.

Wednesday, August 6. The Camp was visited early in the morning with rain, accompanied by thunder and lightning. The company rolled out at 10 o'clock a.m. and, after traveling 5 miles, they crossed the creek where there was no bridge which caused a long detention. The company left the road and camped a short distance to the left on a bottom where the water and grass were good. Day's journey, 11 miles.

Thursday, August 7. The company had to pull up to the main road, and at 8:30 a.m. half the company proceeded on their journey, leaving the other half on the camp ground, on account of some individuals claiming a yoke of oxen belonging to the Church which affair had to be settled. Half the company journeyed 14 miles and went half a mile off the road, where they camped at the bottom of a hill where feed for the cattle was good, but the water was bad.

Friday, August 8. The company started at 9 o'clock a.m. While going up a hill toward the road, Brother Briner's [Bruner's] wagon got into a hole and tipped over; his wife, child and mother were in the wagon, but were not badly hurt, although the bows were all smashed. The distance traveled during the day was 19 miles, but it was nine o'clock p.m. before the whole of the company camped and found sufficient water and feed for the cattle.

Saturday, August 9. The company began to move off the camp ground at 8:30 a.m. and soon all were on the way. Early in the afternoon it commenced to rain very heavily, making the roads very slippery. With great difficulty the brethren succeeded in getting up the hills, of which there had been many since the company left Iowa City. Some of the wagons were compelled to halt and camp before getting up with the main body. The distance traveled during the day was 21 miles.

Sunday, August 10. The wagons which were left behind the previous evening overtook the main train which rested until they all arrived, and as there was good feed and good water the company traveled no further that day. A meeting was called in the evening, when nearly all the visitors had left the camp. Captain Dan Jones had something to tell the company which was absolutely necessary for the travelers to understand, but as only a few attended, he appointed another meeting to be held at 8 o'clock the next morning.

Monday, August 11. According to appointment, a meeting was held at 8 o'clock a.m. Captain Dan Jones addressed the brethren and sisters, showing them their several duties and pointing out wherein they had lacked in fulfilling them, and of their lack of union and unwillingness to do what was required of them. Several of the captains of Tens also spoke and all agreed with Capt. Jones that something must be done. A good spirit prevailed in the meeting and those present appeared willing to answer the calls made upon them in the future. And it was resolved that they would obey their captains, and responded to what might be required of them in the future. It was also resolved that all should give heed to the call of the marshal for guards and <to> look after the loose herd, and to be in readiness for hitching up as soon as the cattle were brought into the corral. Brothers Ferguson, Webb and McAllister arrived in the afternoon. Capt. Jones said that he was <had been> requested to have the company in order, so as to join President Richards' company at Florence, as originally designed, and go through to the Valley by mule trains <teams>. In the evening another meeting was held, at which it was moved that Brother John A. Hunt should succeed Dan Jones to the captaincy of the company. This motion was sustained unanimously.

Tuesday, August 12. Public prayer meeting was held in the camp at 7 o'clock a.m. The company resumed the journey at 10 o'clock, traveled 6 miles and camped on Indian creek. Here the bridge crossing the stream was in bad condition, but the company crossed without accident. Here was a plentiful supply of water and the feed for the cattle was good. George Rust McDonald was re-baptized by Elder John A. Hunt. He was confirmed by Elder James Ferguson the following day. Another meeting was held in the evening, addressed by Capt. Hunt who wished to come to some arrangement respecting the two mules which he said were bought for herding and hunting cattle, one of them being used in hauling <the> smith forge and <the carriage> on which it rested. This was objected to, and the statement made that the meeting had nothing to do with the matter, it being a joint stock concern, in which the shareholders had all the right.

Wednesday, August 13. The morning was wet in the camp which did not move all day. Thomas Parry (aged 21 years) from Wales, died at noon of inflammation of the brain, and was buried in the evening in a burying ground, about two miles from camp. The deceased has <up to the time of his death> served as teamster to Capt. Dan Jones. Up to the time of his death.

Thursday, August 14. Elders Ferguson, Webb, McAllister, and Dan Jones left the company in the morning with their mule teams. The camp started at 9 o'clock a.m. crossed several streams over which the bridges were bad; otherwise the road generally was very good. The leading Ten <(John Lewis, Captain)> camped at 8 o'clock p.m. at a place where there was a creek of <good> water and pretty good short grass for the cattle. The rest of the company camped about 2 miles in the rear where there was no water. The distance traveled <by the main company> during the day was 18 miles.

Friday, August 15. At 9 o'clock a.m. the other Tens resumed the journey, and after traveling 2 miles they passed the Ten which traveled ahead the preceding day, as each Ten took a turn in traveling ahead each day. On reaching the creek on which the first Ten had encamped during the night much time was occupied in watering the cattle, and therefore it was midday before the last Ten had left the creek to proceed on their journey. In the evening the company crossed a river 50 yards wide (Des Moines River) at the town of Fort Des Moines. Capt. Hunt remained at the crossing and assisted <some of> the wagons across with an extra yoke of oxen. It was 10 o'clock p.m. when the whole company got onto the campground, 2 miles west of the town, after traveling 14 miles during the day. At the campground water was scarce, but the feed was pretty good. A number of persons from the town visited the camp late in the evening; they formed a procession and paraded inside of the corral playing on some instruments of music; but they shortly withdrew, not finding much patronage from the company.

Saturday, August 16. The company resumed the journey at 9:15 a.m. rested an hour in the middle of the day and made their evening encampment at 5 o'clock p.m., having traveled 12 miles during the day.

Sunday, August 17. A meeting was appointed for 2 o'clock p.m. and the camp was ordered not to move, because of the wet weather. That meeting was not held, <however,> but a prayer meeting was held at 8 o'clock p.m. where timely instructions were given by

Captains Hunt and Davis. Water at this place was scanty and feed for the cattle not very good.

Monday, August 18. The company proceeded on their journey at 10 o'clock a.m. and traveled without making a noon halt, the greatest part of the way over a level plain. About noon they crossed a river about 30 yards wide, without accident, and formed their evening encampment between 6 and 7 o'clock, having traveled 16 miles during the day. At this camping place the water was good and there was <also> plenty of feed for the cattle. A prayer meeting was held at 8:30 p.m. and instructions given by Captains Hunt and Davis.

Tuesday, August 19. For some time prayer meetings had been held every night and morning in the camp. This morning prayer meeting was over by 7:30 a.m., and the cattle immediately brought into the corral. Three oxen were left in the brush [but] were soon found, when the company was again on the way, traveling over good roads. At 11 o'clock a.m. a creek was crossed, on the bank of which the company nooned. This evening encampment was made on the top of a hill where fuel was rather scarce, but where the water and feed for the cattle was good. In the evening prayer meeting, Captains Hunt and Elder Davis gave timely instructions.

Wednesday, August 20. The company resumed the journey at 8:30 a.m., traveling again over a very hilly country, but the teams got along without assistance, and the wagons kept well together. An hour was spent resting in the middle of the day, and the evening encampment was made between 6 or 7 o'clock p.m. at a place where the water was good, and feed for the cattle found a short distance from the camp. At the evening prayer meeting, Capt. Davis proposed that any man, woman or child who had come to years of accountability, who was found disobeying the counsels or instructions of the captain, should be compelled to leave the company. The camp voted unanimously in favor of the proposition. It was also proposed that any man who was found taking out a gun for the purpose of shooting before the corral was formed, or shooting within half a mile of the camp, should forfeit his gun. This proposition was also accepted by all present.

Thursday, August 21. At 8:30 a.m. the wagons began to draw out, and when four Tens were on the way, it was found that a pair [of] oxen belonging to the fifth Ten had not been brought into the corral, which prevented the rest from starting, and search was immediately made for the missing animals, men being sent out in different directions for this purpose, but the missing oxen could not be found. Capt. Hunt stopped until 5 o'clock p.m. and left word for those behind to work on Sunday and endeavor to overtake the four Tens as soon as possible.

Friday, August 22. Capt. Lewis' Ten was still detained on account of the missing cattle. Further search was made for them up to 1 o'clock p.m. but with no avail. Moses Jenkins, who owned the missing oxen, would be <was> compelled to purchase another pair of oxen at the first opportunity. He made arrangements with a Mr. Osbourn of Dal[?] to have them advertised and gave him authority to sell the oxen, when found, and remit him the cash, after deducting all reasonable expenses. Capt. Lewis' Ten left the campground at 3:30 p.m., traveled 7 miles in 3 hours and camped <at 6:30 p.m.> for the night, where water was scarce, but feed good.

Saturday, August 23. The small company of <nine> wagons left behind the main company resumed the journey at 7:45 a.m., traveled 12 miles before dinner 7 miles after, and camped at 6:15 p.m. at the place where the feed was good but the water scarce.

Sunday, August 24. The journey was resumed at 10 o'clock a.m. The company passed Indiantown at 4:30 p.m., and traveled 5 mi[l]es further and camped at 7 p.m. where water was plentiful and the feed for the cattle [was] very good. Day's journey, 14 miles.

Monday, August 25. The wagons moved off the campground at 9 a.m. and camped just over the toll bridge where they paid 20 cents for each wagon and oxen <belonging>. Here was plenty of water, but the feed was not very good. The distance traveled during the day was 15 miles. Capt. Hunt came back on <from the main company riding> a mule, and met the rear company at 11 o'clock a.m. and he informed the brethren that they were only 9 miles from the main company.

The Captain stopped with the little company until they had passed a small bridge. In going over this bridge Capt. Davis' wagon capsized in the creek, but, as good luck would have it, only one bow was broken. The rest passed over the bridge without accident. Near [the] bridge which was reached after making a steep descent, there was a quick turn in the road.

Tuesday, August 26. The rear company resumed the journey at 8:30 a.m., traveled through a very hilly country, crossed three or four fine streams of water and camped on one of them at 7 p.m., after traveling 18 miles during the day. Here the feed was good. The main company was only 2 miles ahead.

Wednesday, August 27. The small company resumed the journey at 8:30 a.m., passed through Bluff City (Council Bluffs) at 11 a.m., and reached a point close to the ferry on the Missouri River at 6:30 p.m., about an hour after <the arrival of> the main company. The feed here was very scanty. Day's journey, 16 miles.

Thursday, August 28. The ferrying of wagons across the Missouri River was commenced at 8 o'clock a.m., and at 7:30 p.m. the whole company of 56 wagons had been taken across without any serious accident, and camped close to the city of Florence.

Friday, August 29. The company was busy in taking provisions and other requisites for the journey on the Plains. Flour sold at $4.50 per hundred., cornmeal at $2.50 per hundred, sugar, 10 <12> and 15 cents a pound, etc. Very little bacon could be had and most of the company had <only> a trifling weight of it.

Saturday, August 30. A meeting was held in the evening which was addressed by Elder Erastus Snow, who gave instructions concerning the journey. He advised them <emigrants> to stop for nothing, except for resting their cattle, as there was no time to waste. There was no sickness in the camp except a case or two of ague. Notice was given that all who were ready would move their wagons out about three miles from Florence to a place where the feed was better and the rest were to follow as soon as possible. Some of the company decided to stop at Florence. Among them <were> Nathan Davis with two wagons, Henry Dalrymple with one wagon and many others out of the other wagons. Henry H. Wiseman, a son of John and Mary A. Wiseman of Canterbury, England, died, aged two years.

Sunday, August 31. The company commenced to move out of Florence at 8 o'clock a.m. and by evening all the wagons had moved out three miles, where the feed was but middling and the water scarce. A meeting was held in the evening addressed by Elders Erastus Snow and Franklin D. Richards. Elder Snow alluded to the Saints when they were driven and settling down. It was the desire of President Young that settlements should be made all the way between the Missouri River and Great Sal[t] Lake City. There would then have be no need of mules or ox teams, but they <brethren could> would be travel from one settlement to another with their packs upon their backs. He threw out these hints for the Saints to think about, and some [of] them began to wonder if they would be called upon to settle down anywheres on the road.

Monday, Sept. 1. The company remained in camp all day. Some discarded some of their loading, according to instructions. The cattle were brought into the corral for safety.

Tuesday, Sept. 2. The company left the camp around 10:15 a.m., traveled 7 miles and camped for the night at 3 p.m. on the Big Papillion, where there was plenty of good water and good feed. The cattle were brought into the corral for the night.

Wednesday, Sept. 3. The camp got ready and started off at 10 o'clock a.m., and arrived at the Elkhorn River at 1:30 p.m. The wagons were ferried across with as much haste as possible, and by 7:15 p.m. all were across. Traveling 2 miles beyond the ferry, and encampment was made for the night on Rawhide Creek, where water was plentiful and feed pretty good. The cattle were not corralled that day. Distance traveled, 10 miles.

Thursday, Sept. 4. Every exertion was made for the company to start earlier than usual and so they left the campground at 8 o'clock a.m. They found good traveling for 12 miles, and after resting an hour and three quarters near the Platte River, the journey was continued. An encampment for the night was made near a slough had to give water to <where the brethren had to carry water for> the cattle. The feed was plentiful but coarse. Day's journey, 18 miles. Brother William Salisbury's four-year old son was run over by a wagon during the day and seriously hurt; he fell from the seat in front of the wagon.

Friday, Sept. 5. A storm commenced in the camp at 6 o'clock a.m. accompanied by thunder and lightning. It continued for 1 1/2 hours. The company moved at 9 o'clock a.m., stopped 2 hours in the middle of the day and then journeyed until 6:45 p.m., when an encampment was made on Shell Creek, after traveling 17 miles, during the day. The water and feed here was good. During the day, the company met some Californians, who reported that Almon W. Babbitt's company had been attacked by Indians <and> that two men and a child had been killed; one woman was missing, the other two men escaped, leaving the four wagons.

Saturday, Sept. 6. Esther Walters, wife of John Walters, from Cardiff, Wales, was delivered of a daughter at 5 o'clock a.m., and was doing well. The company resumed the journey at 8:45 a.m. Franklin D. Richards, Daniel Spencer and 12 other brethren passed the company with a mule team at 10:15 a.m. <going west>. After traveling 12 miles, the company rested, where these brethren waited for them. They were pleased with the manner the wagon company had proceeded on their journey and gave the brethren every encouragement of success in their further travels. Brother Richards and company left the company and which followed them, 2 hours later. Encampment was made at 6 pm. Three miles from the Loupe Fork ferry on the Platte River bottom, where the feed was good. Distance traveled, 18 miles.

Sunday, Sept. 7. The journey was resumed at 8 o'clock a.m. and after traveling 3 miles, they <company> reached the Loupe Fork ferry, with the expectation of crossing over at once, but the water had risen the night before so much that the tackle belonging to the ferry-boat was damaged, and <making> it was too late for crossing that evening. This gave the travelers and their cattle a day's rest at a place where the feed was good.

Monday, Sept. 8. The wind blew hard and the water was very high in the Loupe Fork. The ferrymen, with the assistance of some of the brethren, got the rope across the river and straightened the same. Brother George Spencer's company of Ten was taken across in the evening.

Tuesday, Sept. 9. The remaining wagons of the company were taken across Loupe Fork, the ferrying being finished at 2 o'clock p.m. A yoke of oxen belonging to the Church was missing and several of the brethren were sent out to search for them; they returned with them to camp at 4:15 p.m. Brother Ellis Jones had lost two gentle cows on Sunday last at the Loupe Fork ferry and up to this time had not been found. The company moved forward at 5 o'clock p.m. and after traveling seven miles camped at 8 o'clock p.m. on the banks of Loupe Fork.

Wednesday, Sept. 10. At 8 o'clock a.m. the wagons left their place of encampment, traveled 13 miles and stopped 2 hours for the cattle to water and feed; then the journey was continued until 7:15 p.m., and a camp made on the Loupe Fork after traveling 20 miles during the day.

Thursday, Sept. 11. The company broke camp at 8:30 a.m., went back half a mile and crossed the hills towards the Platte River, traveling a part of the day over sandy roads. After nooning 2 hours the journey was continued and the night encampment made on a creek where there was also a good spring of water and good feed for the cattle. This camp ground was a quarter of a mile from Loupe Fork.

Friday, Sept. 12. The company started at 7:45 a.m. and traveled 9 miles over a sandy road and stopped to noon. The brethren did not expect to find water, but when a few of the wagons were moving on, and the rest were preparing to do so, a prairie creek was discovered not far off. All hands then stopped and watered their cattle, then journeyed 4 miles further and camped at a place where there were several wells. The feed there was tolerable good, but there was no water for the cattle and no timber.

Saturday, Sept. 13. The company resumed the journey at 6 o'clock a.m., stopped at a pool of water at 8:30, which soon became so muddy that only a few of the cattle would drink it. Having stopped only a few minutes, the journey was continued and Prairie Creek reached at noon. Here the brethren watered their cattle and rested 2 3/4 hours, then traveled 11 miles further to a creek where water was plentiful, but feed rather scarce; but <there was> sufficient fuel. The night encampment was made at 8 p.m. after traveling 22 miles.

Sunday, Sept. 14. The journey was resumed at 9:30 a.m. and the company traveled 2 miles and camped again on the same creek. Here grass was rather short but was sufficient to feed the cattle.

Monday, Sept. 15. The journey was resumed at 8 a.m.; the weather being very hot, the cattle suffered much. At 4 o'clock p.m. the company crossed Wood River on a very rough timber bridge and camped two miles further on the banks of the creek, where the feed for the cattle was good. Day's journey, 14 miles.

Tuesday, Sept. 16. The company started at 8:30 a.m., and in traveling found no water until 4:30 p.m., when the brethren turned off the road half a mile and camped near the Platte River where the feed was good. This place was about three miles past Fort Kearney. Day's journey, 16 miles.

Wednesday, Sept. 17. The company broke camp at 8:15 a.m. A cold, rough wind sprang up and continued the whole day. The company stopped 1 1/2 hours to water and rest their cattle and camped at 6 p.m. on Buffalo Creek. The cattle were kept in the corral all night, there being no feed for them. The distance traveled during the day was 17 miles.

Thursday, Sept. 18. This was a very cold morning in the camp and the company left at 6 o'clock a.m., traveled till 8 o'clock <a.m. or> until they reached a creek where they stopped to feed on the scanty grass. After stopping about three hours, the teams were again hitched up and the company moved on. The night encampment was made on Prairie <a small> Creek at 6 p.m., after traveling during the day 18 miles. At this place feed was rather scarce.

Friday, Sept. 19. The company resumed the journey at 8:15 a.m. In the afternoon, about 5:30, a tire came off one of the wheels of

Sister [Sarah] Taxford's wagon, which detained the company a short time. The camping place being some distance away, the brethren were compelled to leave the wagon on the prairie. After traveling 20 miles during the day, the night encampment was made at 8 o'clock p.m. half a mile off the road toward the Platte River.

Saturday, Sept. 20. This morning a company of armed men returned to the camp <broken wagon on the prairie> with the repaired wheel and the wagon was brought <the wagon> safely to camp. At this time several other wagons in the company had loose tires and the brethren set about <to work> repairing them. They intended to move off in the afternoon and so all the cattle were driven into the corral and yoked up, but as a rain storm approached, the plan was changed, so that no move was made that day. A mail going east crossed to the other side of the river, bringing news from other emigration companies ahead. A company of traders came near the brethren that night as the feed for animals was good.

Sunday Sept. 21. The cattle were again driven into the corral to be yoked up, but on account of a brother who was dying, the camp was detained all day. A buffalo was shot in the afternoon and the meat distributed. Brother Elias Davis from [blank] departed this life at 3:45 p.m. aged 44 years, leaving a wife; he was highly respected by those who knew him. The disease which laid him low was diarrhea. He was buried the same evening by the roadside.

Monday, Sept. 22. The company started this morning at 7:30 a.m. and passed over some sand bluffs at midday. They camped at 6 p.m. on Skunk Creek, three miles from the crossing, where there was good feed and water, after traveling 16 miles during the day. The camp was aroused at midnight by the guards who saw some one walking about, and crossing the corral, and <but> would not answer when spoken to. Nothing further was seen of it, and so the men retired to their beds again.

Tuesday, Sept. 23. The morning was cold and frosty. The company resumed the journey at 6 o'clock a.m. An accident occurred to Sister Ann Davis, whose husband died 2 days before. After crossing

Skunk Creek she was in the act of getting out of the wagon when her clothes caught in the tongue, and she fell; the wheels passed over her thigh and shoulder, but luckily the road <bed> was soft sand and the injuries received were not so serious but that she was able to walk a few hours afterwards. Capt. Hunt and Spencer shot a buffalo in the afternoon which was brought to camp in the evening and the meat distributed. The night encampment was made at 6 p.m. on the Platte River, after traveling 18 miles during the day. The grass was somewhat scarce on this ground.

Wednesday, Sept. 24. Sister Mary Goble, wife of William Goble of Brighton, England, was delivered of a daughter in the morning. The company started at 9 o'clock a.m., traveled until sundown and camped for the night after making the <a> distance of 14 miles. During the day the company traveled over a sandy road. The feed, at this place was <not> good.

Thursday, Sept. 25. The journey was resumed at 7:50 a.m., and as the road led over sandy bluffs, the cattle had a hard time of it. The night encampment was made on the Platte River, but it was after 7 o'clock p.m. before all the wagons arrived in camp, being detained thru the ups[e]tting of Brother Bill's [William Bell's] wagon. The driver ran against the bank of a creek which the company had to cross instead of going over a steep sandy bluff. Sister Bells [Sarah Bell] broke her arm in the accident. Day's journey, 16 miles.

Friday, Sept. 26. The company started at 8:30 a.m. and traveled over a very soft, sandy road, crossing several sandy bluffs, which tried the cattle very much. After traveling 10 miles during the day, the night encampment was made at 6 o'clock p.m.

Saturday, Sept. 27. The company started at 8 o'clock a.m. and traveled over a level country, but through a great deal of soft sand. After traveling 16 miles, encampment was made at 6:15 p.m. where feed was scarce.

Sunday, Sept. 28. The journey was continued at 8:10 a.m. and the road led through considerable sand for 10 miles and then through more sand bluffs. Instead of going over them, the company passed along the bottom, near the river, having to double teams. All got through safely. Traveling some distance further, the night encampment was made at 6:30 p.m., having traveled 12 miles during the day. The feed for the cattle was somewhat scarce. The cattle were corralled.

Monday, Sept. 29. An ox belonging to Elias and Joel Jones was found dead this morning in the corral. It seemed to be in good condition, but ha[d] been strained the day previous. The brethren named had two wagons and did not double their team as <like> the rest of the company did. The journey was resumed at 9 o'clock a.m. and the traveling was over sandy roads, where the pulling was hard part of the day. The evening camp was made at 6:30 p.m.

Tuesday, Sept. 30. The journey was continued at 8 o'clock a.m. The roads during the days' travel, were better, and the encampment was made for the night on the Platte River, after traveling 16 miles. The feed for the cattle was scarce.

Wednesday, Oct. 1. The journey was resumed at 8 o'clock a.m. The company stopped 3 hours in the middle of the day, which was much longer than usual, Captains Hunt and Spencer endeavoring to find out where the others <preceding> companies had crossed. Several sand hills were encountered during the days journey, and the night encampment was made at 6 p.m. where there were some green patches of grass, but otherwise the feed was rather scarce. Day's journey, 13 miles.

Thursday, Oct. 2. The company commenced to cross the [unreadable] at 8 o'clock a.m. and all got across it in about 2 1/4 hours. A company of mule teams, carrying soldiers, etc., bound for Fort Laramie, passed the brethren at 10 o'clock a.m. An hour later, they met a company of people with ox-teams, who were on their way back to the States from Utah and who gave an account of the poverty of the people there. At noon, the brethren met a company of soldiers and mule teams from Fort Laramie. After traveling 13 miles the night encampment was made on the Platte River at 6:30 p.m. The feed at this place was poor.

Friday, Oct. 3. The journey was continued at 8:30 a.m. on a good road. At 6:30 p.m., after traveling about 16 miles, the night encampment was made about 5 miles from Chimney Rock. Two worn out oxen were left by the wayside during the day, but they <one of them> came into the camp at night. The feed at this camping place was better than usual.

Saturday, Oct. 4. Sister Susannah Bruner from Switzerland died somewhat suddenly this morning, although she had been declining for some time past. At 1 o'clock a.m. she asked for a drink, and half an hour later she was found dead. This sister, who was buried at 8 o'clock a.m. was 64 years old. The company resumed the journey at 8:30 a.m., passed Chimney Rock at 10 a.m. and camped for the night at 4:45 p.m. near a place where good feed for the cattle was found on some large islands in the river. Caroline Brenchley was re-baptized by Elder John Cunison for the restoration of her health. Marinda Nancy Pay, daughter of Richard and Sarah Pay, died of diarrhea, just before midnight. She was 10 weeks old. Day's journey, 13 miles.

Sunday, Oct. 5. A company of 20 missionaries and some others who were traveling with them for protection, passed the camp at 10 a.m. with horse-teams, Parley P. Pratt and Thomas Bullock being among the number. The journey was resumed at 3 o'clock p.m., and, after traveling 5 miles, the night encampment was made at a place where feed was scarce.

Monday, Oct. 6. As the morning was very foggy, the brethren found it difficult to find all their cattle, but the journey was resumed at 8:30 a.m. Brother John Turner from Natley, Kent, England, died at 9:45 a.m. of diarrhea, his illness having lasted about four weeks. Brother Turner, who was 42 years old, left a son and daughter of tender years. A tire came off one of the Church wagon wheels which caused some delay. The company passed Scott's Bluffs, traveling over a very irregular, rough road. No noon halt was made that day and the night encampment was made on the Platte River at 4:30 p.m., after traveling 9 miles. Feed was scarce. Ruth Jones [was] born.

Tuesday, Oct. 7. The company resumed the journey at 7 o'clock a.m. An ox belonging to Brother Richard Griffiths gave out. The dead ox was unhitched from its mate and the journey continued with one yoke of oxen. The lo[o]se pair of oxen was left for Brother Samuel Evans to drive, and while driving them, one of the bow keys broke, by which means the oxen became separated and the one that had the yoke hanging to its neck ran off and so frightened some of the other oxen that it caused them to leave the track and go at high speed, wagon after wagon. Soon, however, they were going at a terrible speed in different directions, causing a general consternation. The <people belonging to the> last half of the train was exposed to great danger of being knocked down, or crushed between the wagons. In a few minutes, however, the cattle were brought to a standstill, after some ten or 12 wagons had left the road. During the stampede, Sister Esther Walters from <Cardiff> Wales was knocked down and so badly injured that she expired in a few minutes afterwards leaving a babe four weeks old, which at the time was in the wagon. The remains of Sister Walters were interred in the evening at 5 o'clock. She was 39 years old. After Brothers Goble's wagon (which was broken in the stampede) was repaired, the company traveled on about one mile farther and camped at 6 p.m. Day's journey, 13 miles.

Wednesday, Oct. 8. The journey was resumed at 7:30 a.m. and the company traveled well and without detention all day. Encampment was made at 6:30 p.m. where feed was good, after traveling 20 miles.

Thursday, Oct. 9. The company started at 8 o'clock a.m. The latter part of the day, the roads led over soft sand, and it was with great difficulty that some of the wagons could pull through. The encampment for the night was made at 7 o'clock p.m., about one mile from Fort Laramie, after traveling 20 miles during the day. The feed was very poor at this camp. John Joseph Wiseman, aged 5 years, son of John and Mary Ann Wiseman, died at 10 p.m. from bodily weakness.

Friday, Oct. 10. The camp was visited in the morning by some of the brethren from the wagon and handcart companies, which were only a few miles ahead. The company started at 3 o'clock p.m., traveled over sandy road part of the way and camped at 6 o'clock p.m., after traveling 6 miles. The feed was poor at this camp.

Saturday, Oct. 11. The camp did not move this day, some trading of cattle being done.

Sunday, Oct. 12. Brother [William] Beesley and family with his wagon and Brother [William] Bell and family, with his wagon left camp and started back for Fort Laramie in the morning. The cause for Brother Beesley's return was the weak condition of his team, and Brother Bell did not wish to endure the severity of the weather, journeying so late in the season. The company broke camp at 12 o'clock noon, traveled 7 miles and camped on the Platte at 4 o'clock p.m.

Monday, Oct. 13. The journey was resumed at 8 o'clock a.m., traveling <going> over a very hilly country. After traveling 20 miles during the day the encampment was made at 6:40 p.m., two miles from the river, where the feed was pretty good.

Tuesday, Oct. 14. The journey was continued at 8 o'clock a.m. and after traveling 15 miles during the day, the night encampment was made at 4:45 p.m. at a place where the feed was good across the river. At the evening prayer meeting it was proposed that as James Creek had removed from the Ten, over which he was captain, that John <James> Holley should succeed him as captain of the Ten, and that James Creek <should> assist <Charles> Holley as captain of the guard, in some of his duties.

Wednesday, Oct. 15. The journey was resumed at 8:30 a.m. and the river forded at noon <to the north side>. After traveling 17 miles, the encampment for the night was made at 5:45. Pretty good feed was found across the river.

Thursday, Oct. 16. The journey was resumed at 7:30 a.m., the company again forded the river at 1 p.m. to the south side and the night encampment was made at 7:15 p.m., after traveling 22 miles. Feed was rather scarce.

Friday, Oct. 17. The journey was continued at 8:30 a.m., and the night encampment made at 5:45 p.m., after traveling 16 miles. The cattle were driven across the river to feed on rather poor grass.

Saturday, Oct. 18. The company started at 9 o'clock a.m., traveled 15 miles and camped on the Platte River at 6 p.m., where the feed was tolerably good.

Sunday, Oct. 19. The journey was continued at 7:30 a.m., and Capt. Edward Martin's handcart company was passed just as it was ready to start, after having <it had> stopped for dinner. Many of the handcart people pulled their carts alongside of the wagons belonging to the Hunt company "and", writes the clerk of the wagon company, "it was enough to draw forth one's sympathy for them, seeing the aged women and children pulling their handcarts, many of them showing haggard countenances. We passed Fort Bridge <(Platte Bridge)> about noon and camped at 2 o'clock p.m. on the fording place on the Platte River, after traveling 14 miles. Capt. Hodgetts <wagon> company had just forded when we arrived, and the handcart company crossed directly afterwards."

Monday, Oct. 20. This morning the ground was covered with snow which prevented the company from moving. The cattle were driven into the corral in the afternoon, some 12 or 14 head being missing. It commenced snowing again at 3 p.m. and continued for some time.

Tuesday, Oct. 21. The snow <in the camp> was about 8 inches deep, which completely stopped the company from traveling. The missing cattle had crossed the river and got mixed with Capt. Martin's company. They were all found.

Wednesday, Oct. 22. The fording of the <Platte> river was commenced at 1 o'clock p.m. by doubling teams. <After> traveling one mile on the other side, an encampment was made for the night. The brethren cut down cottonwood trees to feed the cattle.

Thursday, Oct. 23. The weather was very cold and frosty. William Upton who arrived from Capt. Hodgett's company the previous evening by [means of] Jesse Haven to consult Dr. Wiseman, died of mortification of the heart aged 34 years. The camp was still detained because of snow. By this time several of the cattle had died.

Friday, Oct. 24. A very cold north-west wind was blowing, and the snow was quite deep, almost as deep as when it first fell. More timber was cut down to feed the cattle. One ox was found dead, and two more were not <being> able to stand the weather were slaughtered.

Saturday, Oct. 25. The snow drifted by the effect of a cold and strong wind so that the ground became bare in some places, thus enabling the cattle to get a little grass.

Sunday, Oct. 26. There was a slight thaw during the day and the cattle looked much better. Capt. Hunt went to Fort Bridge to see about trading for cattle to replace those that had died.

Monday, Oct. 27. The snow melted gradually. four <six>teen head of cattle were brought from the Fort in the evening and more could be had on the morrow.

Tuesday, Oct. 28. The weather continued cold. Brothers Joseph W. Young and two other brethren arrived in camp in the evening from the Valley. This caused <a general> rejoicing generally throughout the camp, though the tidings of the snow extending westward for forty or fifty miles, was not encouraging. The handcart companies had been supplied with food and clothing and the conditions of the wagon companies would be reported to the Valley speedily, as the brethren traveling in that company <with teams> were also getting short of provisions. Thirteen head of cattle were brought from the Fort in the evening.

Wednesday, Oct. 29. The three brethren, who had arrived in the camp from the Valley the day before, left the <Capt. Hunt's> company on their return, expecting to be back with the help in ten days. The company on their return, expecting to be back with help in ten days. The company resumed the journey at 2 o'clock p.m., leaving <on the camp ground> one old wagon belonging to Brother [James] Walters who had joined Brother [James] Farmer in bringing their teams together and making one wagon serve for both families. After traveling 3 miles a new encampment was made at 3:30 p.m., at a place where the feed was scarce.

Thursday, Oct. 30. The company resumed the journey at 9 o'clock a.m., the weather being fine, but the roads heavy, leading over high hills and wet, sandy ground. After traveling 7 miles, the company went into camp at 2 p.m., near the Platte River, where the feed was scarce. Margaret Price, wife of John Price of Pembrokeshire, Wales, was delivered of a daughter.

Friday, Oct. 31. The company remained in camp all day. The brethren who had received fresh cattle from the traders at Fort Bridge upon a draft of Brigham Young held by Brother Thomas Thomas (who kindly proffered it for the use of the camp) signed bonds, giving <as> security to him of their oxen and wagons.

Saturday, Nov. 1. The company resumed the journey at 11:15 a.m., but traveled only a short distance when a snowstorm came on, accompanied by rain, making the ground very wet and muddy. All the emigrants were cautioned not to the let the cattle drink, as the road led through poisonous creeks of water. After traveling 12 miles, encampment was made at 7 o'clock p.m., where there was no wood nor water. The company was met during the day by Brothers Cyrus H. Wheelock and William Broomhead from the Valley. They came to find out the condition of the wagon company.

Sunday, Nov. 2. During the night a hard frost had prevailed and several of the cattle had strayed away. Search was made <for> some distance around the camp but they could not be found. Those who had their teams traveled on to Willow Springs, from which place oxen were sent back to bring up the other wagons afterwards. Capt. John A. Hunt and Gilbert Spencer went back to the previous day's camping place and found the missing oxen, which they brought to camp late in the evening. At this place, the snow was 6 or 7 inches deep, and the weather was very cold. The brethren cut down willows for the oxen. The company traveled 4 miles during the day. A meeting was held in the camp in the evening addressed by Elders Wheelock, Webb and Broomhead, and a unanimous vote was taken that all the emigrating Saints would be willing to do as they were instructed, even if it was required of them to leave all they had behind and be glad to get into the Valley with their lives only. They agreed to cease complaining at coming so late in the season, as everything was being done to start the company.

Monday, Nov. 3. The company started at 10:30 a.m., the weather being very cold. Fourteen or fifteen oxen were left on the road. The night encampment was formed on Greasewood Creek, half a mile from the crossing, at 8 p.m., after traveling 11 miles, during the day. The infant child of William Goble died at 9 o'clock p.m.*

*From this date on, the camp journal was written with lead pencil which at this late date, Feb. 25, 1926, can scarcely be read. It would appear that the ink used by the scribe had frozen, and the journal from now on contained only a few entries.

Tuesday, Nov. 4. The brethren found some green grass growing along the banks of Greasewood Creek and they scraped off the snow in places, in order to find something for the cattle to eat. A fresh start was made at 3 o'clock p.m., but after traveling 5 miles, another encampment was made on the same creek (Greasewood Creek).

Wednesday, Nov. 5. Jane Walters, daughter of John Walters, died at 9:30 a.m., aged 8 weeks. The company started at 11 o'clock a.m., passed Independence Rock at 2 p.m. and arrived at the log house at Devil's Gate at 8 p.m. Here Brother Hodgett's company were encamped. Brother <George> Grant and other brethren from the Valley were stopping here to give the emigrating Saints instructions in regard to their further journeyings to the Valley. A meeting was called which was addressed by Brothers Grant, Cyrus H. Wheelock and <Robert T.> Burton. Brother Grant informed the emigrants that they would have to leave their goods at this place (until they could be sent for), such as stoves boxes of tools, <spare> clothing, etc., and only take along sufficient clothing to keep warm, with their bedding. He wanted four or five wagons and teams to assist the handcart companies and he expected them to take only about half the number of wagons along. All present expressed their willingness to do whatever was expected of them. The distance traveled during that day was 12 miles.

Thursday, Nov. 6. The weather was intensely cold and stormy and the snow drifted very much. The brethren commenced to unpack their wagons and store the goods in a log house. William Burton died at 10 o'clock p.m. He had been brought down with ague, and could not bear the intensity of the cold. Brother Burton was 26 years old.

Friday, Nov. 7. The weather continued extremely cold. More wagons were unloaded and the goods stored. Ann Davis, aged 47 years, died at 4 p.m. of diarrhea.

Saturday, Nov. 8. Capt. William B. Hodgett's company rolled out from Devil's Gate encampment, and the remainder of the wagons in Capt. Hunt's company were unloaded. An inventory of the goods left at the log house was given to Brother George Grant.

Sunday, Nov. 9. The weather being a little milder, the company resumed the journey at 12 o'clock noon, crossing the Sweetwater and camped at 4 p.m., having traveled 6 miles. Twenty-four wagons were the number taken by the company from Devil's Gate.

Monday, Nov. 10. (Nothing was written in the camp journal this day.)

Tuesday, Nov. 11. Mary Hutchinson, aged 70 years, died at 4 o'clock p.m. James Reese, aged 60 years, died at 9 o'clock p.m. after suffering a long time from diarrhea and ague.

Wednesday, Nov. 12. Sophia Turner, aged 14 years, was found dead in bed, having been suffering with diarrhea for some time past.

Thursday, Nov. 13. (Nothing was written in the camp journal this day.)

Friday, Nov. 14. (Nothing was written in the camp journal this day.)

Saturday, Nov. 15. (Nothing was written in the camp journal this day.)

Sunday, Nov. 16. John Turner, aged 12 years, died at 7 o'clock a.m. of diarrhea.

Monday, Nov. 17. (Nothing was written in the camp journal this day.)

Tuesday, Nov. 18. (Nothing was written in the camp journal this day.)

Wednesday, Nov. 19. The company crossed the South Pass and camped at the Pacific Springs.

Thursday, Nov. 20. The company was divided into several smaller ones.

Friday, Nov. 21. The camp clerk writes: "Four horse teams arrived in camp this morning and took away about ten of our company to each <of their> wagons."

Saturday, Nov. 22. The camp journal says: "A number of Oxen came from Fort Bridger and took one from several of the <of our> wagons to that place."

Sunday, Nov. 23. (Nothing was written in the camp journal this day.)

Monday, Nov. 24. (Nothing was written in the camp journal this day.)

Tuesday, Nov. 25. (Nothing was written in the camp journal this day.)

Wednesday, Nov. 26. The company arrived at Green River.

Thursday, Nov. 27. Sarah Pay, aged 30 years, died of diarrhea.

Friday, Nov. 28. (Nothing was written in the camp journal this day.)

Saturday, Nov. 29. Several wagons crossed Green River and camped on the other side, in order to be in readiness to start on the following morning.

Sunday, Nov. 30. The remainder of the wagons left Green River.

Monday, Dec. 1. (Nothing was written in the camp journal this day.)

Tuesday, Dec. 2. (Nothing was written in the camp journal this day.)

Wednesday, Dec 3. (Nothing was written in the camp journal this day.)

Thursday, Dec. 4. The last of the wagons arrived at Fort Bridger.

Friday, Dec. 5. (Nothing was written in the camp journal this day.)

Saturday, Dec. 6. A messenger arrived from Great Salt Lake City in the evening, bringing intelligence that a number of teams were coming on the road to bring in the remainder of the Saints from the mountains [and] they were also bringing provisions with them. This caused great joy in the camp.

Sunday, Dec. 7. Fourteen wagons <(relief teams)> arrived in camp in the evening from the Valley.

Monday, Dec. 8. More wagons <(relief teams)> arrived in camp from the Valley.

Tuesday, Dec. 9. This morning some of the teams who<ich> had come from the Valley to help [bring] in the belated emigrants started on their return.

Wednesday, Dec. 10. (Nothing was written in the camp journal this day.)

Thursday, Dec 11. (Nothing was written in the camp journal this day.)

Friday, Dec. 12. (Nothing was written in the camp journal this day.)

Saturday, Dec. 13. (Nothing was written in the camp journal this day.)

Sunday, Dec. 14. (Nothing was written in the camp journal this day.)

Monday, Dec. 15. The following is the last entry made by lead pencil in <Capt.> John A. Hunt's camp journal: "The remainder of the saints arrived in Great Salt Lake City today, the emigration being now completed."

Appendix 5

Discourse of Brigham Young at General Conference, 30 November 1856 Reported by George D. Watt in the *Deseret News*, 10 December 1856

I have a few words to say, before this meeting is brought to a close. We expect that the last hand-cart company, br. [Edward] Martin's, will soon be in the streets by the Council House. What preparations the Bishops have made for their comfortable reception and temporary disposal I know not, but I know what I desire and am going to tell it to the people.

When those persons arrive I do not want to see them put into houses by themselves; I want to have them distributed in this city among the families that have good and comfortable houses; and I wish the sisters now before me, and all who know how and can, to nurse and wait upon the new comers and prudently administer medicine and food to them. To speak upon these things is a part of my religion, for it pertains to taking care of the Saints.

We have quite a task upon us this season, for when the last hand-cart company arrives and is comfortably disposed of, we still have about 400 more brethren and sisters who are yet beyond Fort Bridger, probably near Green river. They are those that came out with teams, or the independent companies. All their gold, their silver, their cattle and their other property will not enable them to reach here before the snow has overtaken them; and they had plenty of cattle, of money and means; everything that heart could wish, for an outfit for crossing the plains.

To succor those 400 I call out door business; I call it a snow business, a labor, mountain toil and fatigue of a severe description.

Night before last we received a messenger from those two independent trains, by whom we have learned that they are living on their cattle at Green river. The brethren at Fort Supply are striving to get them as far as Fort Bridger.

Our messengers started out night before last to gather fifty more relief teams. We have sent to Utah and Tooele counties.

Until now, this and Davis and Weber counties have had to bear the burden. We have sent for those teams to carry flour to Fort Bridger, and load back with people. Some, perhaps, will have to be left there, and if so we will carry supplies to them and keep bringing in the people, until all are comfortably provided for.

Those that are yet back have been living probably for nearly a week, solely on the cattle that die; they have no flour, and are subsisting upon cattle that drop down through weakness and exposure, which is certainly hard fare. Still, do not be scared, for they will eat and live and come here.

I can say that the great majority of the brethren here, so far as we have called on them to assist this year's immigration, have freely and nobly manifested their faith by their works. True, some that went out have been imprudent, though I think it will all come out right and I can feel to bless them, notwithstanding they have been imprudent and foolish. I will tell them wherein, when I can have them before me in this congregation.

As soon as this meeting is dismissed I want the brethren and sisters to repair to their homes, where their Bishops will call on them to take in some of this company; the Bishops will distribute them as the people can receive them.

I have sent word to Bishop Hunter that I will take in all that others will not take. I have house room enough to accommodate the whole of them, if it is necessary; I am willing to take my proportion.

The afternoon meeting will be omitted, for I wish the sisters to go home and prepare to give those who have just arrived a mouthful of something to eat, and to wash them and nurse them up. You know that I would give more for a dish of pudding and milk, or a baked potato and salt, were I in the situation of those persons who have just come in, than I would for all your prayers, though you were to stay here all the afternoon and pray. Prayer is good, but when baked potatoes and pudding and milk are needed, prayer will not supply their place on this occasion; give every duty its proper time and place.

This is what I can say truly, with the rest of your counselors and directors, that no man or woman, that we have any knowledge of in the church, has refused to do as requested, with regard to this immigration; they have run by day and night. Our messengers have been traveling from here to the Platte, and back and forth between Bridger, Green river and the Sweetwater; and scores of men have been riding by day and night, without having enjoyed an undisturbed night's rest during the last two months only occasionally snatching a little sleep when sitting by the camp fire. They have been riding by day and night, hurrying to and fro and laboring with their might and have not refused to do what we have required of them; this is to their praise. Works have been most noble when they were needed; we put works to our faith, and in this case we realize that our faith alone would have been perfectly dead and useless, would have been of no avail, in saving our brethren that were in the snow, but by putting works with faith we have been already blest in rescuing many and bringing them to where we can now do them more good.

Some you will find with their feet frozen to their ankles; some are frozen to their knees and some have their hands frosted. They want good nursing, and if you do not know how to treat frozen flesh, let me inform you that the same treatment is needed as in a burn, and by pursuing that method you can heal them.

The Bishops are here, and as soon as the meeting is closed they will meet the company and dispose of them as wisdom shall dictate. And I want you to understand that we desire this people to nurse them up; we want you to receive them as your own children, and to have the same feeling for them. We are their temporal saviors, for we have saved them from death. Br. Chislett, who has just been addressing you, would have been dead long before this, had it not been for the assistance of br. George D. Grant and those who went back with him. The rear companies would never have got over the Rocky Ridge, or seen the upper crossing of the Sweetwater, had they not been helped from here.

Now that most of them are here we will continue our labors of love, until they are able to take care of themselves, and we will receive the blessing. You need not be distrustful about that, for the Lord will bless this people; and I feel to bless them all the time, and this I continually try to carry out in my life. The two wagon companies still out we are sending for, and will supply flour to such as may have to tarry at Forts Bridger and Supply. We do not calculate to have the winter blast stop us; it cannot stop the Mormon Elders, for they have faith, wisdom and courage; they can perform that which no other men on the earth can perform.

Index

Page numbers in *italics* refer to images.

A

amputations, 52, 55, 64, 90–91

B

Babbitt, Almon W., 34
Bailey, Langley, 61, 96
Baker, George, 25n10
Barman, James, 47n35
Barman, May (Mary), 47n35
Beecroft, Joseph, 30
births, on pioneer trail, 35
Bowers, Ashley, 18

Bowers, Caroline "Carrie" Goble, *56*
    age at time of immigration, 1
    birth and death dates of, 31n17
    children of, 59, 95
    freezes feet, 47, 86, 98
    visits mother's grave, 57–59, 92–93
Bowers, Christine, 18
Bowers, Dora, 18
Bowers, Jacob, 18, 19
Bridger, Jim, 34
Brighton, England, 1–5, 23

Brown, J. Robert, 43
Bruner (Bryner), Susannah, 35
buffalo meat, 51
bugle, 34–35, 36
Bunker, Edward, 9
Burton, Robert T., 48

C

Carter, Mary Ann Goble, 6, 64
Carter, Thomas, 6, 64
Council Bluffs, Iowa, 36
Cowdy, James, 34

D

death(s)
    of Edith Goble, 41–42, 98
    of Fanny Goble, 31–32, 78, 98
    in handcart companies, 11–12
    of James Goble, 47, 98
    of Mary Goble Pay, 68
    of Mary Penfold Goble, 38, 54, 82–83, 89, 98
    as part of trail life, 35
Devil's Gate, 46, 47–49, 86
Dunbar, W. C., 27

E

Ellsworth, Edmund L., 8–9
emigration
    and life on pioneer trail, 33–35
    route of, 43, *44*
    to Salt Lake City, 7–10

F

"Farewell, Our Native Land, Farewell," 26–27
"Farewell to Thee, England" (Hill), 27
Farmer, James Morris, 47, 86
Farmer, Mary Ann, 47, 86
Farmer, Mary Ann Biddie, 47n35
fog, 28, 76, 98, 135
Fort Laramie, 33
Fort Seminoe, 48
Fowkes, Mary Ann Ewers, 64n1
Fox, Ruth May, 31n16

G

"Gallant Ship, The" (Phelps), 26
Garr, Abel, 45, 46
Goble, Edith
    birth and death dates of, 31n17
    birth of, 35, 38, 82
    death of, 41–42, 98
    and death of James Goble, 47n35

Goble, Edwin
    age at time of immigration, 1
    baptism of, 6
    birth and death dates of, 31n17
    children of, 59, 95
    freezes feet, 47, 86, 98

Goble, Fanny
    age at time of immigration, 1
    birth and death dates of, 31n17
    christening of, 5
    death of, 31–32, 78, 98

Goble, Harriet (Mary's aunt), 5

Goble, Harriet (Mary's sister)
    age at time of immigration, 1
    birth and death dates of, 31n17
    children of, 59, 95
    loses toes to gangrene, 47n37

Goble, James, 1, 31n17, 47, 98

Goble, Mary Ann Ewers Fowkes, 64n1

Goble, Mary Penfold
    burial of, 55, 91
    conversion of, 6
    death of, 38, 54, 82–83, 89, 98
    faith of, 59, 94
    gives birth to Edith, 38, 41, 82
    grave of, 57–59, 60, 92–93, 95
    and Indian attack, 37, 80
    life in Brighton, 1, 23
    Mary's last walk with, 37, 81

Goble, Susannah Patching, 63

Goble, William
    and burial of Mary Penfold Goble, 55, 91
    conversion of, 6
    and death of Edith, 41–42
    at Devil's Gate, 47–49
    employment of, 25n6
    immigration of, 6, 10, 15
    and Indian attack, 37, 80
    life in Brighton, 1, 2, 23
    life in Utah, 63, 64
    relationship between Richard Pay and, 64–66
    sees iceberg, 28, 76
    travels by ox and wagon, 31, 77, 87

Golconda, 6

Grant, George, 39n33, 45–46, 48

H

handcart companies, 8–12, 14. *See also* Hodgetts handcart company; Hunt handcart company; Martin handcart company; Willie handcart company

handcarts, 8, 10

Hanks, Ephraim, 49n42, 50–52, 88

Hardy, Leonard Wilford, 54

Haven, Jesse, 12, 29, 33

Hill, Emily, 27

Hinckley, Arza, 50–52

Hinckley, Bryant S., 71
Hodgetts, William B., 9
Hodgetts handcart company, 9–10,
  11, 12, 29, 39n33, 45–46
Horizon, 1, 24–28, 29–30, 74–76
Hunt, John A., 9, 36, 46, 57, 92
Hunt handcart company
  arrives in Salt Lake City,
    53–54, 89–90
  camp journal of, 119–44
  comparative chronology of
    other companies and,
    101–17
  deaths in, 11
  Horizon passengers in, 29
  rescue company makes contact with, 39n33, 45–46
  route of, 44
  as symbol of pioneer migration, 9–10
Huron, 28n12

I

Indians, 34, 36–37, 79–80
Iowa Campground, 31–32
Iowa City, Iowa, 28, 30, 98

J

Jaques, John, 25n9, 28n12, 29–30, 31n18, 33
Jenson, Andrew, 50

Johnson, Dan, 50, 51
Jones, Dan, 36n26, 46, 48
Jones, Ruth, 35
Jones, Samuel Stephen, 97–99
Jubilee, 57, 92

K

Kay, John, 27
Keokuk, Iowa, 6
Kimball, Anna Pay, 57, 92
Kimball, Heber C., 51

L

Lajuenesse, Charles, 48
Larsen, Vera Pay, 18
Liverpool, England, 24
Loader, Patience, 42, 48

M

Margetts, Thomas, 34
Martin, Edward, 9, 29
Martin handcart company
  comparative chronology of
    other companies and,
    101–17
  deaths in, 11–12
  Horizon passengers in, 29
  rescue company makes contact with, 39n33, 45–46

Martin handcart company (*continued*)
   as symbol of pioneer migration, 9–10
Matless, Leonard, 6
Matless, Matilda Goble, 6
McArthur, Daniel D., 8–9
McBride, Heber Robert, 25n8
McBride, Peter Howard, 32n20
McMurrin, Joseph, 43
McPherson, Bertha, 60n61
McPherson, Jane Ann Ollerton, 60, 96
measles, 31, 78, 98
medical help, 51–52, 55, 64, 90–91
Mills, Harry, 60n62
mutiny, 25, 98

N

Nadauld, Margaret Dyreng, 61n63
North Platte River, 37–38, 43, 81

O

Ollerton, Alice, 60n61
Openshaw, Samuel, 34
oxen, 31, 31n16, 45, 47

P

Patching, Susannah, 63

Paul, Earl S., 50
Paul, Luna Ardell Hinckley, 50
Pay, George, 68
Pay, Georgetta Paxman, 18
Pay, Marinda Nancy, 35
Pay, Mary Goble, 56, 65, 69
   amputation of feet of, 64, 90–91
   arrives in Salt Lake City, 53–54, 89–90
   autobiography of, 13
   baptism of, 6
   birth and death dates of, 31n17
   childhood of, 23, 74
   christening of, 3–5
   chronology of journey of, 21
   comparison of autobiography manuscripts of, 73–96
   conversion of, 23
   death of, 68
   on Devil's Gate, 47–49
   emigration experience of, 10–13, 15
   encounters difficulties in wagon train, 39
   family of, 59, 94–95
   gets lost in snow, 38–39n32, 42, 83–84
   healing of feet of, 64
   letter to Samuel Stephen Jones, 97–99
   life in Utah, 57–61, 66–68

Pay, Mary Goble (*continued*)
   memoir of, 12–13
   mentioned in Church publications and addresses, 13–14
   recounts journey to Sunday School, 60, 96
   on rescue company, 49, 88
   transcriptions of autobiography of, 17–20
   travels by ox and wagon, 31–39, 77–87
   travels by ship, 24–28, 29–30, 74–76, 97–98

Pay, Phillip LeRoy, 18, 41
Pay, Richard, 43, 64–68, 98–99
Pay, Sarah, 64, 66, 99
Perpetual Emigrating Fund (PEF), 7–8
Phelps, W. W., 26
Platte River, 37–38, 43, 81
Pratt, Parley P., 34

R

Raynolds, William F., 34
Reed, Captain W., 24n6, 25n9, 28n12
rescue company, 39n33, 45–46, 49–53, 88, 104–17
Reshaw's Bridge, 43
Richards, Franklin D., 10–11, 27, 29, 33–34, 45
Richards, John Baptiste, 43, 46

Rogerson, Josiah, 27, 30, 48
Russell Square (Brighton), 2, *3*

S

Salt Lake City
   emigration to, 7–10
   Hunt company arrives in, 53–54, 89–90
   Mary Goble Pay's life in, 57–61
   Willie company arrives in, 49n41

Samuel Curling, 6
Sermon, Elizabeth, 52
shark, 25, 75
Simmonds, Ada, 59n55
Simmonds, Emma Penfold, 59n55
skilly, 49, 87
Smoot wagon company, 10–11
"Song of the Saint," 26–27
Southwell, John, 26, 33, 34–35
stampede, 31n16, 45
steamships, 24n5
Stewart, Elizabeth White, 32n20, 42, 49n38
St. Nicholas Church (Brighton), 3–5
Stoker, Patricia Henriksen, 17–18
Stone, Jonathan, 42, 43, 98–99
storm(s)
   handcart companies caught in, 9–12, 14
   at Iowa Campground, 31–32

storm(s) (*continued*)
    Mary Goble Pay gets lost in, 38–39n32, 42, 83–84

T

Taylor, Steven, 45
Thornton, 29
train travel, 30
Turner, John, 35

U

Utah Territory
    emigration to, 7–10
    Goble family's life in, 63–64
    Mary Goble Pay's life in, 57–61, 66–68

W

Walters, Esther, 31n16, 35, 45
Walters, Jane, 35
Waugh, George P., 29
Welsh company, 8–9
Wheelock, Cyrus H., 26–27, 45, 48
Williams, Ezra Granger, 55, 90–91
Willie, James G., 9
Willie handcart company
    arrives in Salt Lake City, 49n41

Willie handcart company (*continued*)
    comparative chronology of other companies and, 101–17
    deaths in, 12
    rescue company makes contact with, 45–46
    as symbol of pioneer migration, 9
    Thornton passengers in, 29
Willow Springs, 42
Wiseman, John Joseph, 35, 63
Wiseman, Mary Ann, 64n2
wolves, 41–42, 43, 99
Wood, Fanny Goble, 6
Wood, John, 6, 63

Y

Young, Brigham
    and amputation of Mary Goble Pay's toes, 55n48, 64, 90–91
    discourse at 1856 general conference, 145–48
    and emigration to Utah Territory, 7, 8
    and rescue of handcart companies, 11, 50, 51, 53
Young, Joseph A., 45, 46

About the Editor

Clark B. Hinckley earned a master's degree in business administration from the Harvard Business School and a bachelor's degree in mathematics from Brigham Young University. He is a banker by vocation and a historian by avocation and is the son of Gordon B. Hinckley and Marjorie Pay Hinckley (the granddaughter of Mary Goble Pay, whose story is told here). He is the author of *Christopher Columbus: A Man Among the Gentiles* and coauthor (with his wife) of *Taking Off the Tag: A Transition Guide for Returned Missionaries*. He and his wife, Kathleen, their six children, and their twenty-four grandchildren are beneficiaries of Mary's courage and faith.